Champion

Sports Illustrated Winner's Circle Books

BOOKS ON TEAM SPORTS

Baseball
Football: Winning Defense
Football: Winning Offense
Hockey
Lacrosse
Pitching

BOOKS ON INDIVIDUAL SPORTS

Bowling
Competitive Swimming
Golf
Racquetball
Skiing
Tennis
Track: Championship Running

SPECIAL BOOKS

Canoeing
Fly Fishing
Scuba Diving
Strength Training

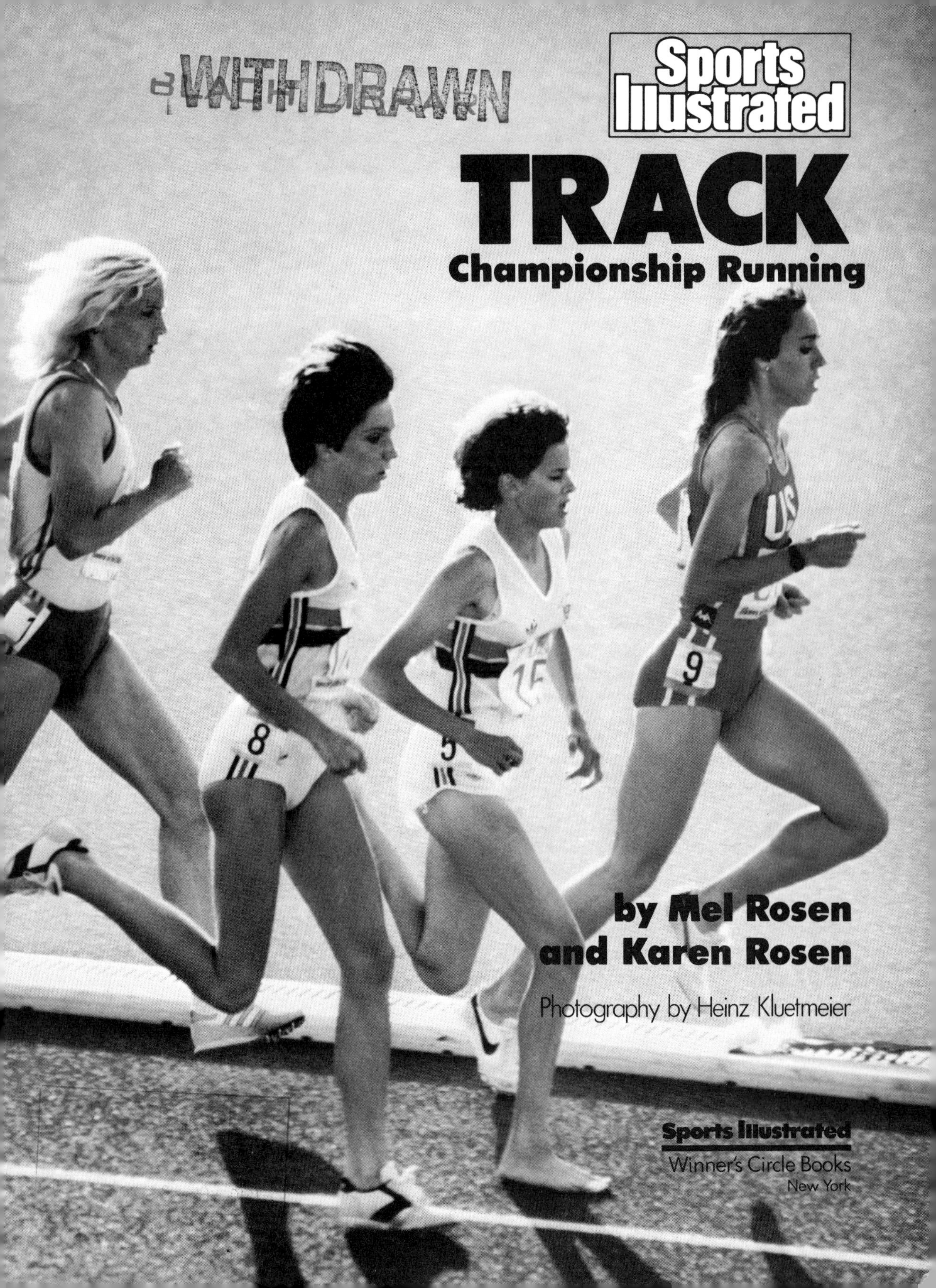

Sports Illustrated

TRACK

Championship Running

by Mel Rosen
and Karen Rosen

Photography by Heinz Kluetmeier

Sports Illustrated
Winner's Circle Books
New York

Photo credits:
Lorraine Rorke, p. 65.
For *Sports Illustrated:* Rich Clarkson, pp. 3, 40, 50, 82, 100, 102, 122, 137, 140; Steve Powell/Allsport, pp. 10, 68, 126; Manny Millan, pp. 14, 70, 80, 91, 125, 129, 138; John Iacono, p. 18; Bill Jaspersohn, pp. 23, 24, 26 (bottom left and right), 114 (top), 116–117; Carl Iwasaki, p. 61; John McDonough, pp. 131, 152; Peter Read Miller, p. 157. All other photographs by Heinz Kluetmeier.
Picture research: Carolyn Keith.
Special thanks to the Golden Eagle Motel, Stowe, Vt.

 For information address Sports Illustrated Winner's Circle Books, Time & Life Building, 1271 Avenue of the Americas, New York, N.Y. 10020.

Designer: Kim Llewellyn

Library of Congress Cataloging in Publication Data

Rosen, Mel.
Sports illustrated track: championship running/by Mel Rosen and Karen Rosen; photography by Heinz Kluetmeier.
p. cm.
Reprint. Originally published: New York, NY: Harper & Row, © 1986.
ISBN 0-452-26105-8
1. Running races. 2. Running—Training. I. Rosen, Karen. II. Title.
GV1061.R58 1988
796.4′26—dc19 87-35610
ISBN 0-452-26105-8 (pbk.) 88 89 90 91 92 AG/HL 10 9 8 7 6 5 4 3 2 1

Contents

Sports Illustrated
TRACK
Championship Running

NIKE
230

1

Introduction to Running

Why do people run? Why do they race against each other? Nobody can tell you why, but both activities seem to be an instinctive part of the human temperament, present in all of us to some degree. Today, literally millions of men and women (and boys and girls) call themselves runners. Some run for glory and championships, some for the thrills of participation and competition, and some just for the fun of it. If you are one of these millions, this book is designed to help you get more out of your running.

Running is a skill. You could just go out and run around the block, but the more skillful you are, the longer and faster you can keep it up. We're not going to give you anything magical or mysterious in this book; we're going to show you the ways that we teach track at Auburn. We hope some points we make will reinforce certain things you're doing now, or maybe give you a few ideas that will make a difference in the progress you are making and help you run more efficiently and effectively.

In a way, the sport of track and field is like an iceberg. Competition is the part of the iceberg that everyone sees, while training is the much larger part below the surface. Keep in mind that for every mile you will run in competition, you will probably run hundreds in training.

Top runners, like Britain's Steve Cram, ultimately run against themselves.

THE PROGRAM

For years, nobody asked me to lecture or write books because the 10.5 second, 100-yard dash man I coached who became a 10.0, 100 man or the 4:40 miler whom I trained to run 4:20 were not nationally known. Then we recruited a 9.5, 100 man who at Auburn improved to 9.0 and a 4:08 miler who improved to 4:00, and people suddenly wanted to know what the Auburn program is all about.

Our program is basically one of *underwork,* even in training for the distance runs. Throughout this book, we will show you workouts that emphasize this point, and, more important, if you follow them correctly, pay off in better times in your event. Over the years we've discovered that the athlete improves just as quickly, but is less prone to injury or burn-out, if he or she saves a little energy for an all-out performance during actual competition. Our theory of underwork is also designed to keep the athlete enthusiastic about practice and about running. Once track becomes a chore, you lose your desire to win. Since most tracks are in meters, we will give all of our interval training in meters. All long runs, which are usually done on roads, fields, or golf courses, will be given in miles.

We don't think there is such a thing as an ideal running events athlete—and that's what makes competitive running such a great sport. Runners come in all shapes and sizes. Sure, at the time he was competing in the Olympic marathon Frank Shorter seemed to be the ideal distance runner because he was lean, moderately tall, and had a good stride and temperament. In distance running, however, there have also been such opposites as Frank Bachelor, who was 6′6″, and Steve Prefontaine, who was only about 5′7″. In the sprints, Carl Lewis is tall and lean while Calvin Smith is small and wiry. Any runner, because of—or in spite of—size can find a niche.

This book is geared mainly toward the competitive athlete, but the recreational jogger or age-group runner, male or female, whose only motivation may be better health, can follow the same ideals and workouts depending on individual talent, interest, and ability.

Some athletes, because they have a preponderance of either "fast-twitch" or "slow-twitch" muscles, seem to be born to run. Physiologists tell us that fast-twitch muscles, fueled by *anerobic energy* (which requires no oxygen), are more suited to sprinting because they contract more quickly and runners are able to attain greater speed with them. Slow-twitch muscles, fueled by *aerobic energy* (which does require oxygen), are more suited to long-distance running because they have more endurance.

Runners come in all shapes and sizes, and any runner, because of—or in spite of—his size, can find a niche.

At Auburn, we try to make athletes winners whether they have fast-twitch or slow-twitch leg muscles. We've heard people say, "My biorhythms show that today's a down day for me, so I can't do my best." But if it's the day of the Olympic final, biorhythms or not, you have to go. It's fine to know about biorhythms, muscle fibers, and the like, but if you're going to be a good runner, *you must cope with reality.* One of the main things we've tried to understand and implement at Auburn is the psychology of what makes people win. *You* know what you want to achieve as a runner (though, if you don't, this book will help you focus your goals). The key, which I stress to every runner I coach, is to *make full and best use of what you have,* during the course of which you will actually improve. In subsequent chapters, we'll examine the key components that can make you a better runner. These components include preparation for running, with a look at equipment, injuries, stretching and diet; endurance training for running; speed training for running; proper running technique; strength training for the runner; and strategy and tactics for every running event. Each of these chapters is designed to help you discover who you are as a runner and then show you how to take what you know to its farthest limits. As you'll quickly discover, there's work involved, lots of it, but then, you wouldn't be a competitive runner if you didn't love to work.

Now, let's get started.

History

By choosing to run, you are entering a continuum that goes back as far as the days of prehistoric man. In a sense, running itself has remained pure, while everything surrounding running—the billion-dollar business of shoes, shirts, and shorts, sophisticated training methods, intercontinental and frequent track meets—has become complicated.

THE ROOTS OF COMPETITIVE RUNNING

In prehistoric days, the fast runner caught small animals for his food and ran away from large animals to live. The swifter he was, the longer he lived.

The swift who excelled in the ancient Olympic Games were rewarded in more material ways. The Games were held every four years, from at least 776 B.C. until A.D. 393, when they were banned by Emperor Theodosius. The Olympics started small, with only one race—a sprint called a *stade,* or 200 meters. The winner was crowned with an olive wreath. Other races up to 4,800

The pinnacle for all runners remains the Olympic Games.

meters and other sports were eventually added, with the winners receiving free room and board for a year; in a way, this was the beginning of the athletic scholarship.

Now we have college athletes running for scholarships and other athletes running for money that is placed in trust funds. Still others run only for health since running is an excellent means of attaining aerobic fitness. The pinnacle for all athletes, however, remains the Olympic Games.

THE MODERN OLYMPIC GAMES

The modern Olympics began in 1896 on a modest scale and have evolved into the present-day Games that include more than 2,000 athletes from 134 countries. In the Olympics, track and field is called "athletics," which is only fitting since it is the purest sport, requiring only that you run, jump, and throw. The Games began with just six running events: the 100 meters, 110-meter hurdles, 400 meters, 800 meters, 1,500 meters, and the marathon. Now, male athletes compete in thirteen running events and female athletes compete in eleven.

At the 1896 Olympics in Athens, Greece, trials and finals were held in most events, but these Games were small-time compared to today's. Now we have four rounds in some events, and events at times stretch over three days. In 1984 at Los Angeles, ninety-six sprinters were entered in the men's 100-meter dash alone.

Each country is allowed one competitor in each event and a maximum of three if their competitors meet a certain standard. In 1984, the United States had fifty-six athletes meet the 100 meters standard of 10.35 seconds, but only three were selected to run in the 100 at the Olympics. In contrast, the 1976 Haitian team was chosen without trials. Haiti's dictator, "Baby Doc" Duvalier, selected his friends and trusted soldiers to compete, but they weren't the country's best athletes and certainly were not world-class.

Not only are the Games the highlight of any athlete's career, but they also tell him if he has reached the top of his event. John Walker of New Zealand, who took the 1976 1,500 meters, had the slowest winning time in an Olympic 1,500 final in twenty years. He wasn't worried that he hadn't set a record in the dull, tactical race. "Every record set in Montreal will eventually be broken and forgotten," he said. "The gold medal is the thing they can never take away from you."

SCHOLARSHIPS

An Olympic gold medal, and even the Olympics, are goals reached by few college athletes, but a scholarship is a goal within reach of many. Thanks to football revenues, each major college or university is allowed by NCAA rules a maximum of fourteen full scholarships per year for its track team, although many schools give fewer scholarships due to scholarship demands in other sports. Scholarships provide an athlete with room, board, tuition, and books. Some talented athletes receive full scholarships; but scholarships can also be divided, and many schools have twenty-five to forty track athletes receiving some aid. Colleges recruit athletes based on their high school performances and offer them one-year scholarships. Naturally, the higher-ranking athletes are awarded more scholarship aid, and some schools adjust this aid up or down each year according to the athletes' college performances.

TRUST FUNDS

There is no doubt in anyone's mind that the athletic scholarship has been a boost to track and field in the United States. Recently, we have had another development, called the trust fund. This fund is controlled by The Athletics Congress (TAC), the official amateur athletic governing body.

The fund works this way: A runner receives a certain sum of money for agreeing to compete in a track meet, and perhaps a bonus for placing first, second, or third. He then takes out his expenses and sends the rest of the money to his TAC trust fund. The same is true when a runner, such as Mary Decker Slaney, Edwin Moses, or Alberto Salazar, endorses a product or does a commercial. After expenses, the runner must send the money to his trust fund. The money continues to accumulate, although an athlete may also draw out medical and living expenses, which are often quite lavish, while competing. Once the athlete retires, he can draw out all his money.

This new rule allows the athlete to keep his amateur and Olympic eligibility. It also has helped the out-of-college athlete compete years after his normal retirement since he can concentrate on training instead of a nine-to-five job. This puts American athletes on a par with runners from Communist countries, who are given stipends by their governments to further their careers.

The jogging craze has spawned serious competitions even for the recreational runner.

THE JOGGING BOOM

Runners who have to earn a living with a nine-to-five job instead of competing in meets have found an outlet in local all-comers meets, in road races, or simply in jogging. The jogging craze began with Major Kenneth Cooper's book on exercise in the late 1950s; his belief that people felt better, looked better, and lived longer by jogging brought on the boom in running. In addition, the expenses are minimal: shoes, socks, supporter for men, shorts, and shirt, and possibly a sweatsuit, depending on where you live.

A SOCIAL SPORT

Running can be a very social sport, whether you run with a school team, a track club, or friends around the neighborhood. You should have team meetings to let everyone know who each of the different people in the group are and to get to know each other and pull for each other. We believe training can be done in groups with a lot of fellowship, but we discourage competition in practice because we practice simply to prepare for races. If you compete in practice, you risk getting hurt, especially if you haven't warmed up enough before giving a hard effort. In a meet you know you're going to give a hard effort, so you're better prepared for it.

The main social values of running include traveling to different places to compete, meeting new people, and learning to deal with victory and defeat. Developing a sense of how to handle yourself as a top athlete in your event, or even less than a top athlete, is equally important, and the self-knowledge and self-discipline that comes through training and competition can spill into other areas of your existence and serve you for life.

Preparation

Proper preparation for competitive running can help keep you going day after day. The more you prepare, the better you feel. In track, the key to success is continuous practice. Any time you miss practice due to injury or other reasons, you fall behind both in your training and in your enjoyment of the sport. Preparation for track includes: (1) using the correct equipment; (2) maintaining a proper diet; and (3) doing the lead-up exercises to everyday training. An easy jog, stretching, an easy workout, and easy weight training help you gradually reach the point where you can endure regular training. Preparation, then, helps you stay healthy and happy.

EQUIPMENT

There are numerous myths about what equipment a runner needs to win a race, but in fact with just a few basics—shoes, shirt, and shorts—he is sufficiently equipped to win an Olympic event. Above all, the uniform must be clean to prevent skin rashes and infections.

Of all the equipment you use, the most important, and the part you should choose most carefully, is the footwear.

Proper preparation for running should always include a passive stretching routine. Avoid "ballistic" stretching—that is, bouncing or jerking movements—at all costs.

Shoes

Even if you run only 15 miles a week, both of your feet are striking the surface countless times a year, which means that—unless you're Zola Budd, weigh only 92 pounds, and are accustomed to barefoot running—you need shoes to protect your feet.

Is a $75 pair of running shoes better than a $50 pair? Running shoes have become a billion-dollar-a-year industry, but costlier doesn't necessarily mean better. When choosing a shoe, let a competent clerk fit your feet, and try on several brands and models until you find a pair that feels comfortable. If you're a jogger or a distance runner, buy a flat-soled shoe with a wide heel; if you're a sprinter or hurdler, buy a shoe with a narrower, less pronounced heel.

You should find a shoe with solid cushioning. The shoe should fit snugly, but shouldn't be tight. To avoid jammed toes, make sure there's room in the toe, about a thumb's width of space between your big toe and the front of the shoe. To make sure the shoes fit, wear to the store the same pair of socks you'll wear when you're running.

Never run in tennis shoes. They have lateral support, which you don't need when you're running forward, but lack the shock absorbency your feet require when running hard. Indeed, running in anything other than a shoe designed for the purpose is an invitation to painful, and often career-shortening, foot injuries.

Once the midsoles of your shoes break down, *buy a new pair.* Don't keep running in the old shoes. Again, you only invite injuries.

Find a shoe with an elevated heel, about three-quarters of an inch thick. Such a heel should relieve some of the strain on the achilles tendon and thus reduce the pressure and shock to the feet of running. Go for a shoe with a waffle or ripple pattern on the sole to provide traction and increase shock absorbency, and stay away from leather uppers, which, unlike nylon ones, tend to trap perspiration rather than "breathe."

You should check to see if your feet have a tendency to roll inwards as they push off. This is called *pronation.* If your shoes are caved in toward the inside, your feet pronate. If your shoes are sloped toward the outside, your feet *supinate,* or land on the outside too much. Check with the shoe salesman to see what kinds of shoes are made to correct these problems; and if the problems are severe, or cause pain when you run, go to a qualified orthopedic physician and have him fit your feet with a pair of *orthotics.* These custom-made inner-soles of foam or soft plastic are designed to compensate for a foot's tendency to pronate or supinate, and though they are expensive—$50 to $200 a pair—they *can* improve your running performance by minimizing extraneous foot movement.

Running Shoes

A good training shoe (A) should be lightweight, have an elevated heel, nylon upper, firm heel cup for lateral support, and some form of waffle or ripple sole (B). Spiked competition shoes, such as those shown here for a sprinter (C), are much lighter and provide less heel support than training models. In addition, the spikes can usually be removed and replaced with a hexagonal wrench (D).

A

B

C

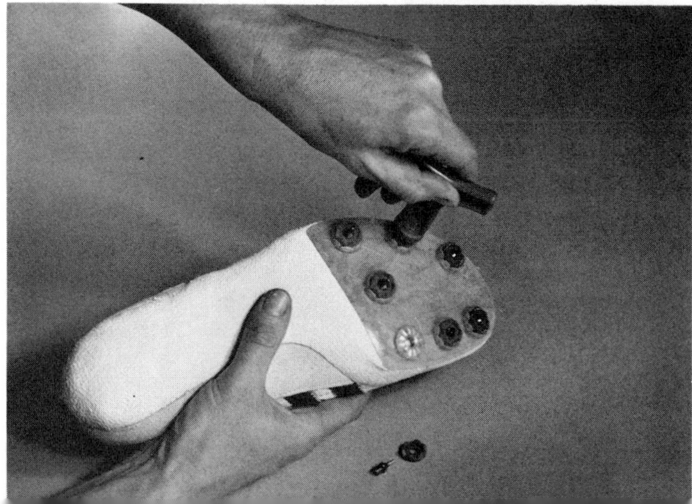

D

Pronation, Supination, Orthotics

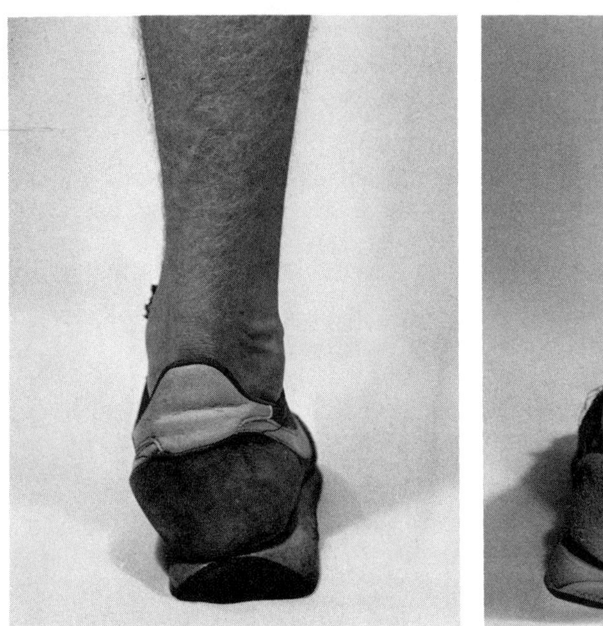

A

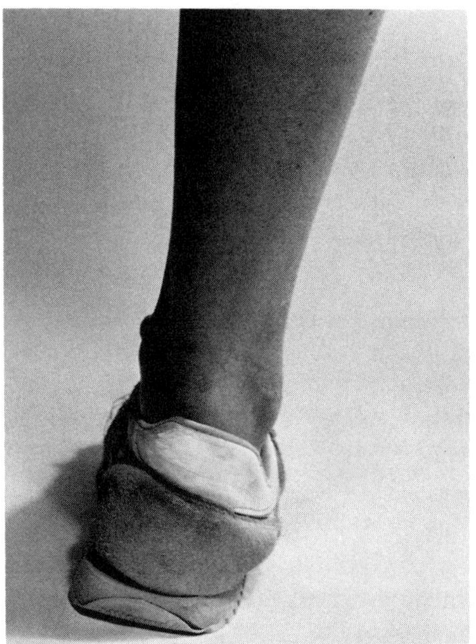

B

Pronation (A), characterized by inward foot roll, and supination (B), characterized by outward foot roll, can often be corrected by wearing orthotics (C), which are foam or plastic insoles custom-fitted to an individual's feet.

C

For competition you should wear a lighter shoe because you are trying for your best performance and you don't want to carry as much weight on your feet as you do when you're practicing. There's also a psychological boost that you gain from running in a lighter shoe; you'll feel that you can run faster without tiring as quickly. Of course, the drawback to your competition shoe is that it gives your foot less protection than the practice model, but on race day you're trying for speed so you have to take that risk.

Never wear the same shoes constantly without washing them, and when you do wash them, follow the manufacturer's recommendations, usually printed on the shoe's inside label.

Unless you are a hurdler, you should always wear flats (shoes without spikes) in practice. Hurdlers may use spikes on days they are doing their technique work over hurdles—set apart at the standard distances—so they can get their timing down. Other runners wear spikes only on competition days, and these lightweight comfortable shoes usually last an eighteen-meet season.

Spikes are removable, and their length depends on the surface. On hard tracks or asphalt tracks, you should use ¼-inch spikes. On softer Rekortan or Tartan tracks, use ⅜-inch spikes because they provide greater digging power. As a rule, the harder the track, the smaller the spike.

Clothing

Most track teams provide their runners with a practice uniform and a meet uniform, each consisting of shorts, T-shirt or mesh singlet (tank top), socks, shoes, and, for men, a supporter. The practice uniform is more durable and easier to wash, while the meet uniform is lighter and bears the team colors. For practice, we always suggest that athletes wear socks to cut down on friction and absorb sweat, and a pair of shorts that have a "V" cut for upper-thigh room.

The chest, torso, and head are the most important parts of the body to be kept warm. You should wear a T-shirt or an undershirt, depending on the time of year and the part of the country you are training in. White, non-porous clothes reflect the sun's rays, mesh lets both sun and air through, and dark colors absorb heat. Of course, we recommend a light sweatsuit for the South and a heavier cotton one for colder parts of the country. Always wear a heavy sweatshirt for warming up and cooling down, and a baseball cap or stocking cap, depending on the weather. Wear a baseball cap when it's 90 degrees outside to protect your head and face from the sun. Joan Benoit wore a painter's cap on her way to the 1984 Olympic marathon victory. Wear a stocking cap when it's 30 degrees or less outside, to keep your head warm: you lose about 25 percent of your body heat through your head. Since your hands get colder than

Track Clothing

Basic clothing for track (A) includes a sleeveless singlet, V-cut shorts, lightweight socks and well-fitting running shoes. For warming up and warming down, wear a sweatsuit, ideally one with a hood (B). A nylon shell and windpants over long underwear or a sweatsuit are ideal for cold-weather running (under 30 degrees) (C). Note, too, the knitted cap and lightweight insulated gloves.

A

B

C

the rest of your body, you should also wear gloves. As a rule of thumb for cold-weather running, if the temperature is *between 30 and 40 degrees,* wear a hat, gloves, and a light windbreaker with shorts. If the temperature is *below 30 degrees,* add legging and a few layers of clothes. And if the temperature is *in the teens,* also wear something over your mouth to warm the air before you breathe it in. Wear bright or reflective clothing if you're running at night.

After running, walk or jog about a quarter of a mile before you sit down or go inside, and once indoors, peel off the clothes immediately. They'll no doubt be wet, and if you leave wet clothes on, your muscles will get sore and stiff.

RUNNING SURFACES

Distance runners and joggers should try to find a running surface that doesn't have too much car traffic. Most likely, it will be a dirt or an asphalt road. We feel that the legs will get accustomed to these surfaces if you start gradually and don't put in too much mileage too soon. In our experience, we've seen many runners suffer foot and leg injuries, including stress fractures, because they tried to do too much too soon on hard surfaces. They lost practice time recovering from their injuries.

If you're a short-distance runner (100, 200, or 400), look for a flat running surface, ideally one made of some type of polyurethane. You should try to do all of your training on this surface *in flat shoes,* as both are easier on the legs.

INJURIES

According to the American Running and Fitness Association in Washington, D.C., one-third of all runners will suffer injuries that will keep them from running for a time. Some runners make the mistake of running on the wrong surface, others don't get adequate rest, and still others don't warm up.

Don't try to run through pain. Stop or slow down if you feel pain of any kind. For years, coaches taught their athletes that pain is something you have to live with and run through, but this is a fallacy. Injuries should be healed or the runner will never recover.

Wade Curington, an outstanding quarter-miler for Auburn in the early 1960s, came to me one day and said, "Boy, my legs feel real good." I said, "What do you mean? Your legs should always feel pretty good." He said, "All through high school, my legs always hurt. I thought this was part of being out for track." I explained to him that the successful runners are the ones who know how to train so that their legs don't hurt all the time.

If a recreational runner seeking conditioning tries to run too much, there's

When training for track, there is a fine line between too little and too much work.

a good chance he'll get hurt. He'll be susceptible to heel bruises, ligament stress, pulled muscles, and achilles stress, to name a few injuries. You might ask, "Why aren't you afraid this will happen to the competitive runner?" We are! But competitors have to take risks, joggers don't.

Anyone who runs 70 to 80 miles a week also runs the chance of messing up his knees and achilles tendons or suffering a pulled leg muscle. Human legs are not designed to take a lot of strain. Your goal as a competitive runner should be to train, stay healthy and yet to do all your workouts. There's a fine line in training between too little and too much work, and our philosophy is that underworking can still mean success. Some athletes believe that if they aren't killing themselves, they aren't accomplishing anything, but we disagree. We've known Olympic sprinters who, during the competitive season, run 2 to 3 miles every morning and then run sprints in the afternoon. We wouldn't change or interfere with their workouts, but we wouldn't let our athletes do them because to run that distance, the runner must land on his heel. Landing on the heel—the so-called "flat landing" in track—is a departure from the sprinter's stride in which only the toes and balls of the feet touch the ground. Sure, long runs are acceptable for sprinters during the fall for conditioning, but they are not conducive to speed, and sprinters should generally avoid them during the competitive season.

Examples of Overwork

Three-time Olympian Harvey Glance, while competing for the South team in the National Sports Festival, was supposed to run the 100, the 200, and the 4 × 100 relay. A few days before the meet, a coach who was working with Harvey and his teammates on baton passes still wasn't satisfied after the twentieth pass. Harvey was getting tired, and on the twenty-first try he pulled a muscle. By trying to make Harvey a little sharper, the coach—and Harvey—lost everything.

The same nearly happened to Evelyn Ashford, the gold medalist in the 1984 100 meters, but she was somewhat luckier. She had been practicing starts before the Olympic Trials 100-meter final and took one too many, pulling a muscle. Many feel she qualified for the 100 on guts. However, Ashford didn't qualify for the Olympic team in the 200. Because she felt a twinge, she pulled up during the 200 semifinal, a race she was favored to win, and left the track in tears.

A muscle pull takes from one to six weeks to heal, depending on the seriousness of the injury, and Evelyn had enough time to recover before the Games. Not every athlete is so lucky, and, from our experience, the ones who overtrain are pressing their luck.

COMMON ACHES AND PAINS

Still, no matter how lucky you are, or how carefully you train, it's inevitable that eventually you'll suffer any of a dozen different common aches and pains. Some, such as stress fractures, are more serious than others, but each of them shares a common characteristic: they prevent you from running your best. What follows is a guide to runner's aches and pains, with recommended treatment for each. Read this section carefully so that you'll remember proper treatment, and keep in mind that nobody can tell you when you're in serious pain—you have to decide that for yourself. Again, running through pain is foolhardy, particularly when, with a little rest and proper treatment, you can be running at full capacity.

Shin Splints

Shin splints are an inflammation in the front of the lower leg and are caused by too much stress and strain on the leg muscles. The problem is common among beginning runners who run on different surfaces and can be extremely painful. You can get over them by wearing well-cushioned running shoes and easing up on your training. If the pain persists, many sports physicians recommend taking aspirin and applying ice to the affected area. You should also do stretching for the shin muscle group (see page 36).

Side Stitches

Side stitches, which can occur during a run, are severe pains below the rib cage in the abdominal area and feel as if a knife is sticking into your body. They occur when the diaphragm is deprived of oxygen. They'll disappear if you slow your pace and use more stomach muscles to inhale and exhale more deeply. You can also squeeze your side as you run, which may relieve the pain.

Heel Spurs

These are bony growths on the heel that cause inflammation and are another stress-related injury. They can be due to flattened feet or overtraining. Stretching exercises and arch supports can help prevent them, but if you do get a heel spur, it will usually go away if you cut back on your work. If that doesn't help, complete rest is necessary, and if the spur still hasn't gone away after six months, it usually must be removed surgically.

Stress Fractures

Also called fatigue fractures or march fractures, stress fractures are small but painful cracks in a bone's structure due to strain, jolting, or pounding. They usually occur in the ball or heel of the foot and disappear after two or three weeks of rest. If you must run with a stress fracture, do so in moderation under a doctor's supervision and only on soft surfaces.

Achilles Tendinitis

This is a swelling and inflammation anywhere along the achilles tendon, which lies behind the ankle and connects the back of the heel to the muscles of the calf and leg. Runners suffer achilles tendinitis when the tendon has been bruised, pulled, or irritated, and it can be prevented by doing stretching exercises with a slant board (see page 36). Like other track people, we treat this and other inflammation-type injuries with ice, knowing that cold forces blood out of the injured area and new blood enters and repairs it when the ice is removed.

Other trainers recommend ice initially and heat later in the course of rehabilitation. For the treatment best for you, consult your trainer or orthopedic physician.

Runner's or Jumper's Knee

Runner's or jumper's knee is a catch-all name for an irritating injury that can be tendinitis, tenosynovitis (inflammation of the tendon sheath), or torn cartilage. Depending on the extent of the condition, many trainers have found that you can still practice and compete with runner's or jumper's knee so long as you warm it up with heat before practice and treat it with ice after practice. It also helps if you take a slow, long warmup and jog before competition.

Calluses

Calluses are rough, thick areas of dead skin on the foot and are usually irritating to run on. An experienced person can shave them down with a razor blade, but caution is essential to avoid cutting live skin. You can also smooth a callus with a pumice stone, but the best ounce of prevention is a good pair of running shoes.

Blisters

These skin injuries, caused by the heat of friction, can be prevented by wearing correctly fitting shoes and two pairs of socks, and keeping your feet dry by sprinkling powder in your shoes. If you get a blister, you should puncture it with a sterile needle, drain the fluid, and try to put some sort of protection around the blistered area, such as a foam donut or gauze and tape.

Lower-Back Pain

Sometimes lower-back pain stems from foot problems: the feet and legs adjust to the problems, but the runner's gait changes, altering the center of gravity in the lower back and causing strain. Adequate stretching can prevent foot problems and, thus, lower-back problems.

Lower-back pain may also come from having weak abdominal muscles, which is why a cornerstone exercise for all athletes is the bent-knee sit-up. A regular regimen of bent-knee sit-ups, along with other conditioning exercises, is an excellent means of keeping both abdominal and back muscles in proper shape.

Arch Problems

If you have trouble with the arch of your foot, such that it is too painful to run on, you should try to get a shoe with ample arch support or see a podiatrist about orthotics. In addition, you can strengthen your arches by rolling a towel in your toes or standing and rising on your toes while turning them inward.

Minor aches, pains, and swelling can be treated by applying ice to the sore area for about twenty minutes, three times a day, and taking aspirin. Harvey Glance is the only four-time scorer in the NCAA 100, partly because he stayed healthy throughout the season by icing down any injury or soreness. We started to wonder if an icepack was part of his body.

Warming up the leg muscles via the whirlpool bath before working out *(left)* and icing them down afterwards with ice packs or ice cups *(right)* can help reduce soreness or injury-related pain.

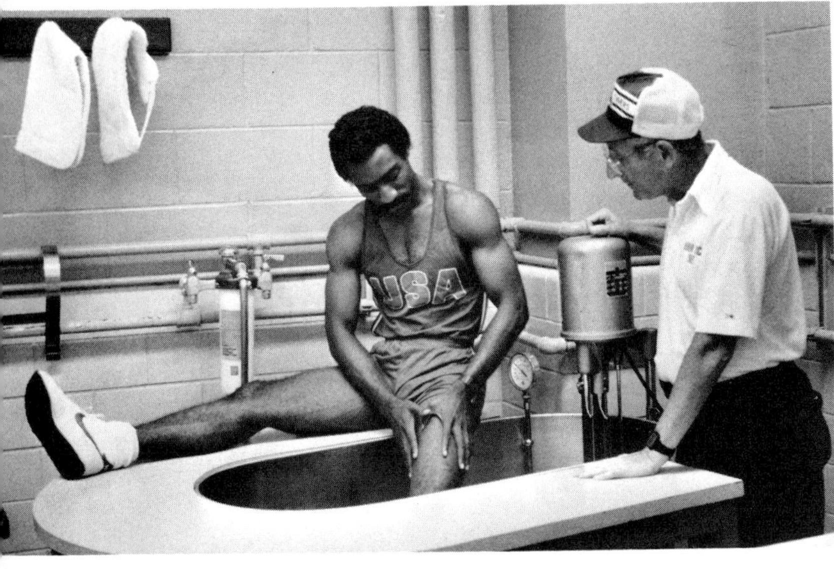

If you're running on a track, alternate the direction you're running to distribute the stress to both feet. It's also a good idea to warm up once every three weeks by running around the track in the opposite direction.

Women sustain physical injuries at the same rate as men. Several studies, however, have found that about a third of all female long-distance runners between ages twelve and forty-five have menstrual problems, including being unable to menstruate. Reasons for this may include loss of body fat, intensity of training, and hormonal changes, but inability to menstruate is not harmful and usually corrects itself when heavy running stops. If they are worried, however, these runners should consult a doctor.

STRETCHING

Stretching helps an athlete achieve a greater range of motion, which will help achieve maximal stride length. At Auburn, our runners stretch before and after practice. Since athletes come in all shapes and sizes, stretching can become one of the great equalizers. Stretching allows the tighter, more heavily muscled athlete to gain greater flexibility and, thus, greater leg speed.

Some athletes are naturally more flexible than others, so they may need only a ten-minute session. Others need more time to limber up to the same degree.

Stretching to Prevent Injury

Stretching is one of the best methods of keeping an athlete flexible and injury-free. Slow joggers who reach toward their toes twice before running may have no problems because they're just shuffling along. By contrast, competitive runners going at a faster pace must put in five to fifteen minutes of stretching to prepare their muscles for any hard effort.

Remember never to stretch out a cold muscle. Stretching is not a warmup, but rather requires its own warmup. We suggest 800 to 3,200 meters (about two miles) of jogging, then ten to fifteen minutes of stretching. You should next take four wind sprints of 100 meters each and you will be ready for your workout or competition. This warmup should become a habit and should be done the same way every day. The jog is really a slow shuffle to get the body moving. The stretching exercises should be done in a steady, static manner, rather than in quick, bouncing motions. Never bob, and always hold each position for at least eight seconds.

Static Stretching
As part of the warmup, track athletes do different types of static stretching. Each stretch should be held a maximum of eight seconds. No bobbing!

Recommended exercises—some of which are illustrated—include these:

1. Standing, with knees locked, reach down slowly and touch your toes. Straighten. Repeat, for a total of six times. This exercise stretches the calf and hamstring muscles, which are susceptible to pulls and tears.
2. Standing, with feet spread and knees locked, hold ankles for eight seconds. Repeat, for a total of six times. This exercise also stretches the calf and hamstring muscles.
3. With the body in a lunging position, reach out to the ground and hold your position for eight seconds. Repeat, for a total of six times. This exercise also stretches the calf and hamstring muscles.
4. With the body in the "hurdler's stretch," lean over and hold your position for eight seconds. Repeat, for a total of six times. This exercise also stretches the hamstring muscles.
5. Assume the "inverted bicycle stretch position," and do this six times. This exercise stretches the upper and lower back, the hamstrings and the neck.
6. Assume the "cobra stretch position," and do this six times. This exercise stretches the lower back, the lumbar area, the abdomen, and the lower rib cage.
7. Assume the "pretzel stretch" position, and do this six times. This exercise is for the lower back and side of the hips.
8. Do the slant board stretch six times. This exercise stretches the tendons and muscles in the heel and lower leg.

Stretching

The Cobra Stretch
This stretches the lower back, lumbar area, abdomen, and lower ribcage.

The Inverted Bicycle
This position stretches the upper and lower back, the neck, and the hamstrings.

The Pretzel
This exercise stretches the lower back and sides of the hips.

Stretching (Cont.)

The Slant Board
This exercise stretches the achilles tendons and the calf and hamstring muscles.

The Hamstring Stretch I
This exercise stretches one of the runner's most important sets of muscles, located in the back of the thigh.

The Hamstring Stretch II
Besides the hamstrings, this exercise stretches the muscles of the lower back.

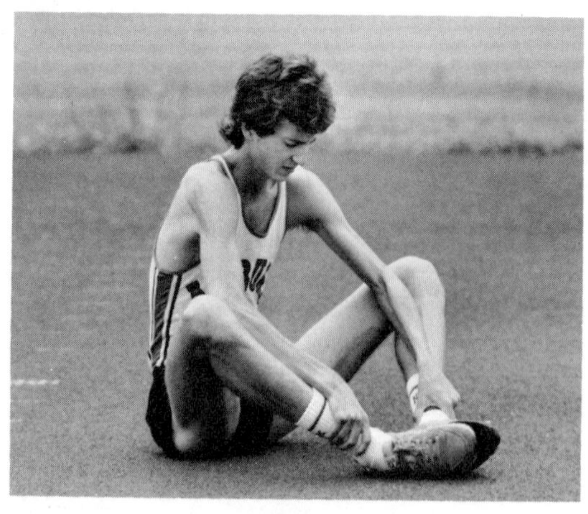

The Groin Stretch
This exercise stretches the muscles and tendons of the groin and inner leg.

Note how the slant board and both hamstring stretches help loosen the leg muscles, while the cobra, the inverted bicycle stretch, and the pretzel all work the upper body.

After a day's workout, always finish by jogging 800 meters, then doing some slow, easy stretching as part of your cooldown, or warmdown. This helps prevent sore, stiff muscles the next day.

DIET

We believe that before a practice session most athletes can eat whatever they want, so long as it doesn't hamper their individual performance. In fact, we've seen athletes come out chewing candy bars or sweet rolls and drinking soft drinks five minutes before practice and not have any distress. However, we've also seen athletes eat the same foods two hours before competition and get sick. Therefore, before practice or competition, you should stay away from foods that are hard to digest, such as milk or chili, and stick to simple, balanced meals.

You should eat about four hours before competition so that you will have time to digest the food. But note: athletes who choose to eat six, seven, or even eight hours before competition may feel weak. They should eat some food before competing, but it should be easy to digest and a small portion.

At Auburn, we've never worried about what our athletes eat, particularly our sprinters; our main concern is the time when they eat, relative to practice and competition. We do feel that distance runners benefit from a high-carbohydrate diet, and, though joggers don't have to worry about the strain of competition and nervousness, they will feel better if they follow the distance runner's diet.

High-Carbohydrate Diet

A high-carbohydrate diet, rich in foods such as spaghetti, baked potatoes, pizza, and salads, plus food from the Basic Four food groups of milk, meat, fruits and vegetables, and grain, along with proper training, will sustain the long-distance athlete. Sweets—such as honey, sugar, soft drinks, or chocolate—that are eaten or drunk an hour before competition may cause a reaction called hypoglycemia, or low blood sugar. This can cause a rundown feeling during competition, so instead of last-minute sweets, what you should count on is the energy from food eaten days, and sometimes weeks, in advance.

Diet for the Distance Runner and Road Racer

While preparing for a road race, eat fruits and vegetables and drink fruit juices. Research has found that tea and coffee, which contain caffeine, can improve endurance in events lasting longer than two hours, such as the marathon. Drinking tea or coffee about an hour before the event stimulates the use of fat, rather than carbohydrates, as a fuel. That saves the stored glycogen in the muscles for longer performance. But caffeine also causes an increase in urine production, which can lead either to dehydration or a mid-race pit stop. Grete Waitz is infamous in Bedford-Stuyvesant after an unscheduled break she took in the New York City Marathon a few years ago.

Pit stop or no pit stop, during a road race you should drink eight to twelve ounces of liquid every ten or fifteen minutes, and even fifteen minutes before the race. Take cold drinks or chew ice. They won't cause cramps or stomach upset, but they will reach the plasma-depleted blood faster and refresh the body better than fluids at body temperature or warmer. Dilute commercial drinks, such as orange juice, with water. The sugar in the fluids may taste good, but, undiluted, can cause cramps.

Don't wait to get thirsty. Your body usually loses two to four pounds of fluid before thirst gives the body a signal that it needs fluid.

You also lose important minerals, particularly potassium, when you sweat, and these need replacement as much as fluids do. There are several brands of "electrolytic" drinks on the market, containing potassium and other minerals; if you use them, it's best, again, to dilute them with water so that the body can absorb their mineral content in less-concentrated amounts.

A simpler way to replace lost minerals and meet other nutritional needs is by eating properly and taking a daily vitamin supplement. Many foods, such as bananas, are high in potassium, and a single multivitamin tablet can contain all the vitamins and most of the minerals you need daily. Note the words "single multivitamin tablet." There's generally no need to take more. In fact, large amounts of certain vitamins, such as A and D, can be extremely toxic.

Gaining Muscle Weight

Extra calories are needed to gain weight as muscle, but they should come from the Basic Four food groups. You need heavy workouts, including weight training, to increase muscle growth and strength. You do not need excess protein.

Steroids—drugs that increase muscle bulk—should never be used. Not only are they illegal in track circles, but, more important, they have dangerous side effects, including stunted growth, acne, deepening of the voice, and altered sex organs. No matter what you may hear or think otherwise, the dangers of steroids far outweigh any possible benefits. Play it smart and stay away from them.

GETTING READY

Getting ready is done before the race, during the week. The great athletes, the winners, know they have done everything possible to be ready for the race.

Now it is time to relax and get your mind set on what you're going to do once the race begins. You should visualize the race itself, your strategy, how you will react to the starter's gun, and, most important, you should concentrate on giving your best effort.

At the 1984 Olympics, the sprinters from the United States—Carl Lewis, Sam Graddy, and Ron Brown—each believed he could win the 100-meter dash and earn the title "Fastest Man in the World." As the U.S. coach, I didn't tell any one man that he wouldn't win. I didn't care in which order they finished, so long as they were 1–2–3.

Throughout the training period, these athletes had worked together as a relay group, but they had then gone their separate ways while preparing for individual races. They trained in exactly the manner they had throughout the year, with their own workouts—why change what had proved successful for them? I just timed them when they asked me or gave them starts, but it was always one at a time. They knew that their top competition was from their teammates, so they avoided each other.

All three made it through their trials and quarterfinals with ease, but in the semis, Lewis won, Graddy was second, and Brown fourth in his heat. I became a little concerned about Graddy and Brown. I went to the room where they were resting while waiting for the final later that night, and, to my surprise, all three were lying in beds side by side staring at a television set. I asked them if they were ready for the final. Lewis quietly said yes, Graddy said he had eased up in the semis to save his energy for the final, and Brown said that he was feeling fine, that a nagging knee injury wasn't bothering him. I wished them all good luck and went to my seat in the stadium.

The final results are history. Lewis was first, winning the first of his four gold medals, Graddy was second after leading for 60 meters, and Brown just missed a medal, placing fourth. Later in the week, they worked as a team with Calvin Smith and set a world record in the 4 × 100 meter relay with a time of 37.83. The great ones know how to get ready.

Preparation's reward: Carl Lewis winning the 100-meter dash at the 1984 Olympics in Los Angeles.

The next story illustrates how not to get ready for the mile relay. In the 400-meter dash of the 1977 Auburn–Alabama dual meet, Joe Coombs of Alabama was in Lane 4, Willie Smith of Auburn, now a three-time Olympian, was in Lane 5, and Darrel Gaston of Alabama was in Lane 6. Coombs went out very hard and came by the 200-meter mark ahead of Smith. Coombs' split was 21.0 with Smith at 21.7, but Smith came back and won the race.

When I approached Willie afterwards, he was really spent and could hardly talk. He started mumbling that he couldn't run the mile relay and was really beat. Suddenly, the announcer said, "In a new stadium record, the fastest time of the year in the world, the winner is Willie Smith in 44.73." Willie jumped up and waved to the crowd and recovered faster than anyone I've ever seen. He did complain to me afterwards that early April was just too soon to run that fast. I said, "Next time, I'll put sand in your pockets to slow you up." I really feel that if you are ready and if the conditions are right, you may run a great one, so why hold back—no matter what time of year it is? In fact, if Willie had approached the race that way, he might have realized that 44-flat was within his grasp.

Back to the mile relay: Willie ended up not running anyway. He talked and talked to his teammates and to the press, and the more he talked, the more excited he got. All of a sudden he passed out. He hyperventilated. As the mile relay—the last event of the meet—began, Willie was being carried to the training room. He looked up and said, "I'm sorry I can't help you." We lost the mile relay 3:08.4 to 3:09.6, partly because a 49.0 man had to substitute for Willie's 44-flat. Auburn wound up losing the meet 78–77. A great performance had cost Auburn a meet because Willie got excited thinking about what he did and what it meant, rather than forgetting about it long enough to prepare for his next event.

As you can see, preparation for running is a process that should begin even before the first day of practice and carry you right to the moment you step to the starting line in actual competition. By following the workouts, getting rest, staying healthy, and keeping in the right frame of mind, you will be prepared for success.

TDK
464
TDK
243

Endurance

Although speed is the most important ingredient for success in running, without stamina work there is no background for the runner, or what is known as "bottom work." We believe in aerobic training as the source of bottom work for all runners. It is done in the fall and builds endurance by developing the runner's lungs, heart, and legs so that he can handle the rest of the program. Further, we encourage aerobic training in our runners in the fall so that they can last a whole season, which normally runs from January to June. Once we get into that competitive season, we run to win and the training is not nearly so endurance-oriented.

We do no speed work in the fall. At that time we're simply trying to get in as much mileage for endurance as we can. Sprinters and hurdlers hate to run long distances so we try not to make them too unhappy, though we know the distance work is ultimately necessary for them to win. It's easier to give the middle-distance runners and distance runners long runs because they enjoy them, but we have to be careful they don't suffer injuries. They also compete in the cross-country season, which is important for two reasons: (1) it gives them a background for the regular winter-spring track

Distance runners in particular need to build their endurance in order to be competitive in their events.

Hill Running
An excellent means of building stamina, hill running should be part of any track athlete's preseason conditioning program. Note the exaggerated arm action and high knee lift when running up steep hills.

season, by making them compete at a five-mile distance, and (2) it is a competitive sport, and thus helps distance runners maintain a competitive edge.

Hill running and bounding drills are often done during the fall conditioning, or preseason, program. Hill training should be limited to uphill running, however, since downhill running can lead to injuries.

ENDURANCE TRAINING FOR SPRINTERS AND HURDLERS

Distance running helps sprinters and hurdlers psychologically because they know they have put in the necessary endurance work in the fall. A good distance base for sprinters and hurdlers is *eight weeks,* enough time so they are in condition.

Besides building their endurance, distance running helps sprinters and hurdlers learn to keep their form even when they become tired (more on form later). Good form is tough to maintain when you are fatigued. In the fall at

Auburn, we incorporate form drills, such as single-file running, to help enhance quality form. We start by running four athletes at a time next to each other, then two at a time, then every runner single file so we can check his form against that of the rest of the runners.

We also have our sprinters and hurdlers (indeed all our runners) do something commonly known in track as *interval training.* Interval training has been the key to my success and the success of thousands of other coaches throughout the United States. It is done by setting up a distance, usually 200 to 600 meters, the time you should take to do the distance, the number of times you should do the distance, and the amount of rest between intervals. For example, a typical endurance-oriented interval program in the fall for college-level sprinters and hurdlers might be:

Week	Distance	Time	Number	Rest
1	400 meters	90 seconds	5	5 minutes
2	400 meters	80 seconds	5	5 minutes
3	400 meters	90 seconds	8	5 minutes
4	400 meters	90 seconds	5	3 minutes

Interval Training
Another means of building endurance, and also improving speed, on-track intervals force the runner to "overload," or do his hardest workouts.

We begin with 400 meters at 90 seconds because we want the sprinter or hurdler to be able to handle initial interval workouts comfortably. Gradually, however, when he is in better condition, he will be able to do each of the same five intervals in 75 seconds, perhaps with rests of only three or four minutes.

The interval approach was first introduced by the Germans in the early 1940s. Their original idea was to run a distance at a certain speed such that the heart rate reached 180 beats per minute. When the heartbeat drops to 120 beats per minute, the runner runs again. When, within a fixed time, the heartbeat doesn't drop to 120, the runner stops the exercise. Today, from experience, most American coaches have come up with their own systems.

Initially, interval training should be done every other day, and each day should be done at different distances so that the runner doesn't get stale. The example above shows different methods of intensifying the workout from one week to the next, which, in track circles, is known as "overloading" the runner. Every week the runner changes one of the variables so that the interval is more taxing and the runner handles more and more stress.

There are numerous different ways to use intervals to condition a runner. Some coaches recommend more runs. We recommend six to eight runs maximum, while gradually cutting down on the rest periods. Why? We have found that this approach generally helps, no matter what the event, all our runners build more endurance over a given length of time than any other approach. Every coach, however, has his own theory of what conditions the runner. In the case of our program, we feel that by the end of eight weeks of interval and distance work, the sprinter or hurdler is in excellent condition and ready to begin his speed work, where the intervals are usually shorter and faster.

ENDURANCE TRAINING FOR MIDDLE-DISTANCE AND DISTANCE RUNNERS

Middle-distance runners build up endurance by putting in more mileage than the sprinters and hurdlers, though following similar workout patterns, and either competing with the cross-country team or training in the regular fall program.

Distance runners definitely put in the long running, and their season normally begins in late July. If they run a competitive cross-country season, they must have 10 weeks of training before the first meet. We believe they should run from 50 to 70 miles a week. Included in the total mileage are the daily two-mile jog to warm up and the two-mile warmdown, in addition to the interval-training workout.

For all athletes running 800 meters or more, we suggest you do intervals one day and a long run the next. In other words, go hard/easy, hard/easy (or, as some runners say, light/heavy, light/heavy). The interval day is hard, the long run is easy. Saturday is the end of the weeklong cycle and the testing day, whether the test is by time trial or meet. Sunday is a very light day, when sprinters and hurdlers take long walks to keep their legs limber, and middle-distance and distance runners take easy runs.

Hard Day/Easy Day Preseason Training
For the runner competing in the 800 meters or longer, alternating hard days with easy days is the best preseason training.

Typical Fall Workout for Middle-Distance and Distance Runners

Sunday No morning workout; afternoon: easy 12-mile run, then weight training.

Monday Morning: 4 miles easy; afternoon: 4 × 1,600 meters, each in 5 minutes with an 8-minute jog between each 1,600.

Tuesday Morning: 4 miles easy; afternoon: easy 7-mile run at 7-minutes-per-mile pace, then weight training.

Wednesday Morning: 4 miles easy; afternoon: 3 × 1,200 meters in 3:30 with 5-minute jog between each run, and 4 × 400 in 62 seconds with a 400 jog in between.

Thursday Morning: 4 miles easy; afternoon: 6-mile run at 6:30 pace.

Friday No morning run; afternoon: jog 5 miles over cross-country course.

Saturday Cross-country competition.

As you can see, this workout schedule is geared for the middle-distance and distance runner who is participating in fall cross-country competition. The workouts combine endurance running, interval running, and easy running (a few days before the meet) to prepare the runner for an all-out effort on Saturday. If you choose to follow this schedule in the fall, you should adhere to the pattern of workouts but pick up the pace on a weekly basis so that your performance from one Saturday to the next will improve. With a little thought, you can tailor a fall program to your own goals and needs, but the above should at least give you a schedule for which days to work hardest and which to ease up.

ENDURANCE TRAINING FOR COMPETITIVE JOGGERS

If you are a competitive jogger, you should follow our workouts but regulate them according to your condition and ability. We believe everyone can do the workouts we have set up, but the key is the speed at which you run them.

Typical Workout for the Competitive Jogger

Sunday No morning workout; afternoon: 8 miles easy, then weight training.
Monday Morning: 2 miles easy; afternoon: 4 × 1,600 in 6:40 with 8-minute walk between intervals.
Tuesday Morning: 2 miles easy; afternoon: easy 6-mile run at 9-minute pace, then weight training.
Wednesday Morning: 2 miles easy; afternoon: 3 × 1,200 in 4:30 with a 5-minute walk in between, 4 × 400 in 75 seconds with a 400 jog in between.
Thursday Morning: 2 miles easy; afternoon: easy 4-mile run at 8-minute pace.
Friday No morning run; afternoon: jog 5 miles over course.
Saturday Competition.

ENDURANCE TRAINING FOR RECREATIONAL JOGGERS

The recreational jogger should take an easy three-mile run every day or mix it up with very slow intervals, such as 6 times 400 meters, each in 90 seconds with a 5-minute rest between intervals.

Runners who have put in the hours at endurance training are better able to maintain good form to the finish.

Endurance training of one kind or another is the basis of success for all runners during their competitive seasons. You cannot begin your speed training or generally expect to run fast without having the stamina to do so. Thus, the fall, or at the latest, early winter, is the best time to start endurance training in preparation for the spring competitive season. No matter when you start, however, *you must put in eight weeks of endurance training before beginning speed work.*

2
3
4
5

Speed

Speed consists in getting from one place to another before someone else—it's that simple. No matter what event you are in, you must develop speed because it will help you win your race, whether it is the 100 or the 10,000 meters. How do you develop speed? Some coaches feel it is simply by doing speed work—that is, running fixed distances either as fast as you can or within fixed times, then repeating those runs after a short rest before the body has a chance to recover fully. *In general, speed work places stress on the body, forcing it to adapt to running faster and faster speeds over given distances.*

And yet, over the years at Auburn, we have learned that *sprinters* will run their best if they are *rested.* Therefore, we recommend *undertraining* sprinters and refraining from having them run full speed too often throughout the training period. In general, we have found that the best way to build up a runner's speed is to make sure his legs stay fresh. Easing up keeps the bounce in the legs, and strength, essential for speed, comes from weight training.

Speed work is applicable to middle-distance and distance runners, too, but the specifics of their speed workouts differ from those of the sprinter's because they are training for greater distances and

No matter the distance, speed helps win races.

rely on *endurance,* fueled by aerobic energy, more than *speed,* fueled by anerobic energy. If, for example, as a distance runner you did the same speed workouts as a sprinter or a hurdler, your speed in the 100 would improve, but your endurance would suffer, so you must hit some sort of happy medium. Ultimately, as a distance runner, you shouldn't worry about your sprinting or "kick" speed as it's called. Instead, you should concern yourself with expending your energy during competition such that you are competitive throughout a race. In the last 100 meters, if you lose in the kick-out, don't be upset, so long as you've worked hard and are spent at the finish line. Distance runners should never sacrifice endurance for speed.

Incidentally, the only times you should go full speed in practice are during starts and wind sprints. (More on wind sprints as part of the practice routine on page 66.) If you are a sprinter, you should definitely try to go full speed during starts and wind sprints because you need some full-speed running to let your muscles experience what they'll be doing on competitive days. In general, however, you'll discover that three-quarters to nine-tenths speed in practice is fast enough for developing good technique and increasing leg speed and keeping the risk of injury to yourself low.

We recommend that distance runners do as sprinters and hurdlers, and work on their form regularly, since good running action is the key to speed. Remember, if you try too hard, you "tie up"—your muscles get tense, your arm action changes, and you slow down. The runner who wins is the one who maintains form the longest. Watch any 400 meters race. Notice that *all the runners will slow up* in the last 60 meters. The winner is the one who slows up the least.

Athletes in any sport have the ability to run fast. The one with the best time in the 100-meter dash is called the "world's fastest human"—until someone runs faster. At the end of 1985, that title belonged to Calvin Smith, the world record holder in the 100 meters at 9.93 seconds.

We have seen short, stocky athletes, tall, lanky athletes, and medium-sized athletes—black and white—attain this renown. Therefore, no person, race, or body build has a lock on this term.

HOW TO DEVELOP SPEED

There are two ways to develop speed that any runner can work on: (1) You can move your legs faster, or (2) you can lengthen your stride while maintaining full sprint power. If you can do both, you may become the world record holder, but usually an athlete can do only one of these things well.

How to Develop Speed
A runner develops speed either by moving his legs faster or by increasing his stride length while maintaining leg power. Few runners can do both things well.

Stride length can be increased by improving leg flexibility and motion range, but from years of coaching experience, we have concluded that this is a poor way of increasing speed. Why? Because lengthening the stride often leads to *overstriding,* with a subsequent loss of speed and a risk of injury. Every athlete has an optimum stride length depending on height. Once you've found yours, the best way to run faster is to work on your *leg speed turnover*—that is, the speed at which your feet touch the track.

You can increase your leg speed by making your muscles stronger, and that includes both leg *and* arm muscles. The faster you pump your arms, the faster your legs will move. Arm and leg strength can be developed in the weight room (more on weight training for speed in Chapter 7).

You must also work on *reaction,* because the faster you leave the blocks the closer you put yourself to the finish line. The better the position you are in when you leave the blocks and the sooner you get into your best position for running fast, the faster you will go. *Good running form contributes to faster leg turnover.*

A

B

C

D

Good Form for Speed
Note the good arm action, straight-ahead toe position, and low knee lift of Olympic gold medal winner Harvey Glance in full stride. A runner's stride is generally 7 ½ to 8 feet, depending on his height. Never overstride!

POINTS TO REMEMBER

Certain points should be stressed about the mechanics of good sprinting, which, of course, is when a runner can move fastest:

1. *Good arm action:* The arms should move straight ahead and not across the body.
2. *Correct position of the feet:* The toes should point straight ahead.
3. *Low knee lift:* This contradicts some experts, who favor an exaggerated high knee lift. We believe, however, that low knee lift gives the athlete contact with the ground more times. This quicker turnover causes you to run faster as you push off the ground more often.
4. *Smoothness and relaxation:* The runner should be relaxed from the neck to the toes, particularly in the neck and shoulders.
5. *Normal breathing pattern:* The runner should avoid holding his breath while he runs.
6. *Good forward trunk position:* A slight forward lean is necessary, especially when accelerating out of the blocks.

Try running slowly in place in front of a full-length mirror to practice all of these techniques.

FORM DRILLS FOR BETTER SPEED FOR SPRINTERS AND HURDLERS

Form drills are designed to keep you sharp and allow you to work on a specific area where you might be weak, and thus hamper your speed. The three most common form/speed drills for sprinters and hurdlers are: (1) knee lifts, (2) quick steps, and (3) kick backs. In effect, these three drills comprise the sprint stride broken down into three parts.

Knee Lift

This drill works toward achieving a full range of leg motion and allows you to work toward your maximum effective stride length. Do knee lifts slowly, concentrating on the rhythm of your arms in coordination with your legs. To do knee lifts, simply run a short distance, raising each knee alternately to waist level. Remember, your toes should point straight ahead and your arms should move straight ahead, too, not across your body. We recommend doing knee lifts four to six times at a distance of 50 meters.

The High Knee Lift Drill
This drill can help you achieve fuller leg motion and optimum stride length for faster running. Note the good arm action and the lift-off from the toes.

A

B

C

The Quick-Step Drill
This drill teaches you to move your feet faster and make more contacts with the ground.

Quick Step

This drill produces quick foot turnover and contact with the ground. The feet should not go much more than two inches off the ground during the drill. To do the quick-step drill, move both your arms and legs in a rapid-fire, vigorous action for 10 meters, then jog the next 10 meters, and repeat twice more. Do this drill four to six times. The best time to do this drill is when you are returning to the starting blocks after a practice start.

Kick Backs

Kick backs are an exercise designed to stretch your legs back as you sprint, and you should concentrate on trying to hit your buttocks with the heel of each foot. As you run, lean forward slightly; this allows you to reach back, yet still turn over quickly. Do these four to six times for 50 meters.

The combination of all three drills can help you increase your stride length to its natural limits, develop fast foot action, and improve your reaction time. They can be done immediately after the warmup or when returning to the blocks between practice starts (see pages 81–88).

Form Running

This can also be thought of as a drill. We line up our sprinters single file so that they can watch each other and learn from each other, and thus become more aware of and concerned about their own and others' running technique. For 50 meters, each sprinter concentrates on foot placement, arm action, knee action, body lean, and relaxation. We do this six times as part of the daily warmup before moving into the full workout session.

Naturally, every coach has his or her own favorite drills, usually similar to these or involving some kind of bounding. We try to find drills that the athletes enjoy, that contribute to their well-being, and yet develop their speed.

Remember, no drill work should be done without an easy warmup and some good static stretching first.

Form Running
Running single file, these runners concentrate on good form: correct foot placement, arm action, and body lean. Both athletes are up on their toes and show perfect knee lift. By running together, they learn from each other.

EARLY (INDOOR) SEASON SPEED TRAINING FOR ALL RUNNERS

Preseason training helps any sprinter, middle-distance runner, or distance runner gain endurance and learn to maintain form. We don't try for speed during that period so much as we try for smoothness and form. Again, our athletes never go full speed except in starts and pickups, but rather go three-quarters or nine-tenths speed. You should work more on starts in the early season, then, as you begin to speed up your workouts, gradually cut down on quantity and go into quality by the late season. (By "quality," we mean running fewer intervals at faster times and taking more rest between intervals. For example, instead of running six 200s in 28 seconds with three minutes of rest between, you would run three 200s in 25 seconds with eight minutes of rest.) Once you do your base work in the fall, you can go into your competitive season doing such speed work, confident you have established a solid base.

During the early season, which for us begins indoors, some of our training changes. We do no long running except on Mondays, feeling that this will help the sprinters when they move up to the 100 and 200 meters from the 50 to 60 meters they run indoors. To get ready for 50 or 60 meters, you need only work on endurance one day a week—usually 300 meters maximum—and you should do this early in the week, preferably on Monday. (This goes back to the premise that as a sprinter you need life in your legs for competition, so after Monday's endurance run, limit your distances to shorter intervals, such as 150s and 60s). You should do as little running around curves as possible since change of direction may cause injury. Top athletic trainers believe that most pulled muscle injuries occur because of a change in weather, loose footing, or a change in running direction—in other words, from running fast on a straightaway to running fast on a curve—so avoid curves in practice if you can.

Before workouts, warm up slowly and cool down afterwards by jogging 800 meters. Weight training (more later) is not as intense as during the fall, but is continued on a maintenance basis throughout the competitive season. If you run the 400 or the mile relay, you should incorporate extra 300s into your Monday workouts and 200s into your Wednesday workouts to condition yourself for those longer races.

Anybody running competitively, be it at the Olympic, intercollegiate, high school, or age-group level, should do basically the same kinds of speed workouts. The only difference is that each athlete should take workouts according to overall ability. If you are a 44-second, 400-meter man, then your Monday 600 meters should be run in 1:24, remembering, of course, that this is nine-

Olympic-level workouts are for Olympic-level runners. Attempting them as a lower-caliber runner can only lead to setbacks.

tenths speed. If you are a 50-second, 400-meter man, then your 600 should be 1:28; if 55 seconds, then 1:34; and so on. Unless you are a top-caliber runner, do not make the mistake of believing that if you do the Olympic champion's workout, that you will run as fast as the Olympic champion. If you try the Olympic champion's workout, then you'll be running all-out and more than likely always fatiguing yourself in practice. That should not be your goal, and from experience we find that if you fatigue yourself in practice, your performance in a meet will be poorer.

Willie Smith, a great Auburn sprinter who was an alternate on the U.S. 4 × 400 meter relay team in 1984, was as fast as guys doing harder workouts. Willie undertrained, which was a plus for us because we never had to worry about Willie getting hurt, unless he was hurt in a meet. One of our goals is to never lose an athlete in practice.

Improving in practice should not be your goal as a runner. Your goal should be to improve on competitive days. Remember: if you maintain your conditioning, if the competition and track are right, and if you push yourself hard, your performance will automatically be better.

EARLY (INDOOR) SEASON INTERVAL TRAINING FOR ALL RUNNERS

Interval training is an integral part of a track athlete's program both during the off-season and throughout the competitive season. The difference, however, is in the interval's purpose. During the off-season, as we saw, the interval was used primarily to build a runner's *stamina.* Now, as he enters the competitive season, the interval is used primarily to improve the runner's *speed.* The key to a successful transition from interval training for endurance to interval training for speed is to start with light workouts in the early (indoor) competitive season and gradually build up their intensity. You do that in one of three ways: (1) by doing more running, (2) doing it faster, or (3) taking less rest. Here is an example of interval training designed to improve a runner's speed, one that can be adjusted to suit anyone's ability. It outlines an early (competitive) season interval program for a 400-meter man whose best time in the event competitively is 50 seconds, and who has progressed during the fall to doing 400-meter intervals at 75 seconds per interval. Now that he is into the competitive season, he does his interval work only once, or, at most, twice a week, cutting the time and distance for the second workout in half.

For example, three weeks of interval work done once a week, would be as follows:

Tuesday	Distance	Time	Number	Rest
1	400 meters	75 seconds	5	5 minutes
2	400 meters	75 seconds	8	5 minutes
3	400 meters	75 seconds	10	5 minutes

Note how this program "overloads" you from week to week by gradually increasing the number of times you run over the whole season, and with one change occurring each week. For variation, you can make the times faster from week to week—say, from 75 seconds to 72 seconds to 70 seconds—or you can cut down the length of the rest period from five minutes to three minutes to two. Note generally, though, how only one variable changes from one workout to the next and how changing that variable intensifies the workout, and thus elevates your speed.

If you find that an interval workout is too easy, then the following week you should overload—that is, you should increase the distance or volume of the workout or reduce the time for each interval—a little bit more than you had planned. You can tell how easy or hard the workout is by how fatigued you feel at the end of practice or how well you handled the workout. If you cannot maintain the pace, the workout is too hard, and if you have to ease up to maintain the pace, the workout is too easy.

Any interval workout program for speed should begin at a pace you can handle and, depending on how fast you get into condition, should become progressively harder. After a certain point, however, you should *maintain rather than increase* the workout's intensity, because, if you overload too much, particularly if you are a sprinter, you will become fatigued.

Here are three examples of interval workouts—over a four-week period, one per week—for a sprinter who can run a 400 in 62 seconds.

Tuesday	Distance	Time	Number	Rest
1	400 meters	90 seconds	5	5 minutes
2	400 meters	84 seconds	5	5 minutes
3	400 meters	80 seconds	5	5 minutes
4	400 meters	76 seconds	5	5 minutes

In the above case, you would run faster each week. In the two following examples, you would increase the number of repetitions in the first case, and decrease the amount of rest in the second.

Tuesday	Distance	Time	Number	Rest
1	400 meters	90 seconds	5	5 minutes
2	400 meters	90 seconds	8	5 minutes
3	400 meters	90 seconds	10	5 minutes
4	400 meters	90 seconds	12	5 minutes

Tuesday	Distance	Time	Number	Rest
1	400 meters	90 seconds	5	5 minutes
2	400 meters	90 seconds	5	4 minutes
3	400 meters	90 seconds	5	3 minutes
4	400 meters	90 seconds	5	2 minutes

This is interval training, and after experimenting with each pattern, you should pick the one you feel will get you in the optimum condition for greater speed—by increasing the number of repetitions, decreasing the rest, or increasing the pace.

Here is an example of intervals for the competitive distance runner.

Tuesday	Distance	Time	Number	Rest
1	800 meters	2:20	5	5-minute jog
2	800 meters	2:15	5	5-minute jog
3	800 meters	2:10	5	5-minute jog
4	800 meters	2:05	5	5-minute jog
1	800 meters	2:20	5	5-minute jog
2	800 meters	2:20	8	5-minute jog
3	800 meters	2:20	10	5-minute jog
4	800 meters	2:20	12	5-minute jog
1	800 meters	2:20	5	5-minute jog
2	800 meters	2:20	5	4-minute jog
3	800 meters	2:20	5	3-minute jog
4	800 meters	2:20	5	2-minute jog

As you can see, the same principles for interval training hold true for the distance runner; only the time, number, and rest variables are different. Indeed, no matter what your running capabilities are, you can tailor an interval program to them such that, if the program is properly followed, you will develop the speed to run your event faster and faster.

Remember: Any interval program you create should last at least eight weeks, and you should start gradually so your legs don't get sore. After the first week at an easy pace, start to intensify the intervals.

FARTLEK TRAINING

Fartlek is a Swedish term that means "run as you feel" or "speed play." This is change-of-pace training worth incorporating into your program any time of the year, particularly the fall and early winter season. One way of doing it is to cover as much distance as you can in forty to sixty minutes. If you feel good, you can sprint for two or three minutes, then jog if you feel tired. Fartlek training is much easier for experienced runners than for novice runners because novice runners often don't know how to change pace. Fartlek training can be a very invigorating kind of workout if done once a week with no set pattern, and it can help you avoid staleness or burnout.

Fartlek Training

A

B

C

Fartlek running is an enjoyable free-form method of training, involving running at varying speeds over varied terrain. In this sequence the runners are striding hard on a flat section by a lake (A), running easily over uneven terrain in the woods (B), running hard up a hill (C), and maintaining a strong pace over the crest of a hill (D).

D

IN-SEASON SPEED TRAINING FOR SPRINTERS AND HURDLERS

Once the regular track season begins in the spring, speed training for the sprinter or hurdler approaches full quality and intensity and typically consists of: (1) six 30-meter dashes from the blocks at full speed to improve starting ability; (2) wind sprints or pickups, starting slow and gradually picking up until the sprinter goes full speed for 30 meters (to improve acceleration); and (3) six 150-meter runs at seven-eights speed to force the sprinter to hold form while tired. Although 150 meters is long enough to really work a sprinter or hurdler yet not exhaust him, we also run 300 meters sometimes to make the runner concentrate on keeping his form over a longer distance. Some sample regular-season workouts for sprinters and hurdlers may be found in the appendix of this book, but for now, let's look at one of the workouts' chief components, the wind sprint.

Wind Sprints

Wind sprints, sometimes known as pickups, can be one of your most effective workouts if you're a sprinter or hurdler because they teach you the acceleration skills needed for better speed in actual competition. To perform a wind sprint, stand at the top of the curve on a typical track and start running slowly.

Speed Training
As part of speed training, the sprinter or hurdler makes six 30-meter dashes from the blocks at full speed.

Gradually pick up the speed until you are in the middle of the track, and then run full speed for another 30 meters. Slowly decelerate to a jog, which should bring you to the end of the straightaway. Walk to the curve and repeat the run on the opposite straightaway. Continue in this fashion for four to six laps, or eight to twelve pickups. Good wind sprint workouts improve acceleration as well as speed and, since they allow little rest between sprints, develop the body's tolerance to anerobic stress.

IN-SEASON SPEED TRAINING FOR MIDDLE-DISTANCE AND DISTANCE RUNNERS

We follow many of the same principles for the middle-distance and distance runner that we followed with sprinters and hurdlers. In speed training in general, our goal is to maintain efficient running no matter at what speed, so the workouts must be hard, long, and varied enough to force the runner to concentrate on this goal.

In the end, efficient running is a matter of speed achieved through correct form, and it is just as applicable when running 10,000 meters as sprinting 100 meters. Indeed, any race begins at a good pace and those runners not strong enough to hold the pace throughout the race drop back. Only the fittest runners remain at the end, and the one who keeps the most efficient running form through to the finish will win the race, just as in a sprint.

Throughout the training year, you should hold many of the same concerns about warmups, warmdowns, drills and stretching as a middle-distance or distance-runner that you hold as a sprinter or a hurdler. During your early (indoor) season work, you should make sure each week includes one day of sprint drills and pickups and keep speed training in your program every week of the year to keep your body accustomed to speed. A body that gets too accustomed to running slow all the time, as can happen especially to distance runners during the off-season, will have a more difficult time making the transition to increased speed work in the winter or spring. Indeed, a cardinal rule of the middle-distance or distance runner is: *Always keep your speed ready.*

Once you are into the springtime competitive season, there are some basic guidelines you should follow as a middle-distance or distance runner. First, besides speed, you also want *quickness*—the ability to accelerate or quicken the pace at will. Second, besides these and endurance, you want *strength.* We use the Monday workout as a speed-strength day and the Wednesday workout as

Reserve Speed

Reserve speed is every runner's ally, as Mary Decker Slaney shows in this exciting finish of the 1983 1,500 meters at Helsinki. Note that by breaking form and lunging toward the finish, her opponent gave up any opportunity to win the race.

a speed-quickness day. Each workout varies as to the racing schedule and stage of the season, but the Monday workout normally ranges from 600 to 1,000 meters with several intervals in between. These are followed by a number of shorter, quicker repetitions—usually between 300 and 400 meters. The speeds for each workout distance are determined by the runner's competition times. If he is a world-class runner, his speed is increased; if he is a novice, his speed is reduced. Let's say, for example, that a runner's best time in the 800 meters is 2:04—far from world-class. He would thus run the Monday workouts at his race pace *plus* a few seconds. In the case of 600 meters, it would be 93 seconds (his 800-meter race pace) plus, say, three seconds, for a total workout time of 96 seconds. For the 1,000 meters workout, the race pace would be 2:38. Add to that, say, two seconds and the total workout time for the 1,000-meter run is 2:40. The speeds are adjusted the next week according to how well the runner handled the workout, and the Wednesday workout is shorter and faster, with intervals of 400 to 600 meters, followed by 150s, 200s, or 300s, depending upon the runner's level of fatigue.

If you are a middle-distance or distance runner training for speed, you should try to keep forty-eight hours between your hard practice (speed) sessions, as well as between your races, to allow your body enough recovery time between hard efforts. If you compete on Saturdays, for example, think of Sundays, Tuesdays and Thursdays as recovery days after hard workouts or races, and on those days limit yourself to easy distance and drill work (the light-day, heavy-day approach, remember?) During most weeks, Friday will be a travel day or light preparation day before competition. To tailor a program to your needs and abilities, look at the sample workouts in the back of this book. As you'll see, they alternate light days and heavy days and incorporate a variety of speed work with endurance training.

As a distance runner training for speed, you should train in much the same manner as the middle-distance runner, only you should vary the interval distances run to be more in line with the length of your races. Your Monday workout might be repetitions from 800 to 1,600 meters (rather than 600 to 1,000 for the middle-distance runner), while Wednesday might be 400 to 800 meters (rather than 400 to 600 for the middle-distance runner). You should also do more mileage than the middle-distance runner on the recovery days. The speeds at which you run the various distances depends on your conditioning and ability. The point to remember, no matter what your event, is that you can always run faster—but you must work at it.

USA
915

Technique

Technique is one of the keys to successful running because no matter how hard you work, if your technique remains unsound, you will make less progress than you would if you had better form. In this chapter we will discuss proper running technique, as well as technique for hurdling—a specialized area of running—and for starts.

No matter whether you are a sprinter or a distance runner, the running technique, in broad outline, is the same: (1) your feet should point straight ahead (though if you're a sprinter, you run on your toes and if you're a middle-distance or distance runner, you land on the balls of your feet); (2) your arm swing should be constant—straight ahead if you are a sprinter and only slightly across the chest if you are a middle-distance or distance runner; (3) your arms should not swing too far back, because that's wasted motion; (4) you should not clench your hands, but cup them; (5) you should keep your neck, jaw, and shoulders loose and relaxed.

Carl Lewis shows perfect form as he rounds the curve toward the finish in the 200 meters. Note Lewis's open hands; most runners keep their hands loosely cupped.

The Sprinter's Stride

Sprinters should stride forward, but neither chop their stride nor overstride. At Auburn, our sprinters usually have shorter strides than other sprinters, for we concentrate on leg turnover—that is, trying to get the feet down as quickly as possible, since the more steps you take at a given stride over a given time, the faster you will go. As discussed earlier, you run faster by taking long strides or more strides. We have always trained our sprinters to go for more strides, and the chief way they achieve this is by concentrating on swinging their arms faster. Of course, stride length, which is defined as the distance between the touchdown of one foot to the touchdown of the other, will vary with the size of each athlete and during the various phases of a race. The stride cadence, which is the number of strides per second, is usually 4.5 to 5.0. With all else being equal, the sprinter who can pick up that cadence will win any race.

The Sprinter's Stride
The knee lift is high, the stride full and directed forward, not up or down. When running at full speed, top sprinters take between four and five strides a second.

A B

The Distance Runner's Stride
A distance runner's stride is shorter and more relaxed than a sprinter's, and the knee lift is lower.

The Distance Runner's Stride

If you're a distance runner, your stride should be economical, according to your height. Remember: Never overstride; instead, try for a comfortable stride and rhythm.

THE FOOT PLANT

The Sprinter's Foot Plant

The sprinter plants his foot with his toes hitting first, then lands on the outside ball of the foot, rolls to the heel, flattens the arch as his weight is absorbed during the full-support phase, rolls back to the ball, and pushes off the inside of the foot at the big toe. This entire motion takes place in a fraction of a second; in effect, the sprinter is relaxing his weight back until his heel barely touches the ground.

The Distance Runner's Foot Plant

Because of their higher mileage and training load, middle-distance and distance runners should run less on their toes, and settle more on the back of their feet to cushion the number of times the feet hit the ground. Ideally, the distance runner should hit on the back of the foot, just forward of the heel, and roll through the ball of the foot and push off. The runner should emphasize spring, rhythm, and a light touch in the foot action. Sometimes it makes sense to shorten the stride length to get quicker turnover. As well, the distance runner should try for a more erect carry of the body than the sprinter, keeping the center of gravity over the powerful upper leg muscles. The body should be totally relaxed and moving efficiently.

ARM ACTION

The Sprinter's Arm Action

Great sprinters run with their shoulders level, allowing their arms to pump freely straight ahead and swing out, down, and back from the shoulder. The arms act as pistons that drive the upper body straight ahead and form approximately a 90-degree angle at the elbow. As a sprinter's arms pump rapidly ahead and back in a push-pull movement, the elbows remain relatively close to the sides to prevent the arms from flapping. As the arms pump forward, the hands go no higher than the head, lest part of the momentum generated by the pistonlike pumping of the arms be dissipated upward rather than continued forward. As the arms pump backwards, the hands go no farther than the hips before they begin their forward thrust. Both hands are loosely cupped rather than tightly clenched (though some sprinters, such as Carl Lewis, prefer to keep their hands open. Either hand position prevents tension and tightness from being transferred up the arms to the shoulders and upper body). All action should be directed forward, not sideways, so that the upper body doesn't zigzag and waste energy. The faster and more efficiently the arms pump, the more the sprinter's legs do the same. As we'll see when we study hurdling technique, beginning on page 92, the hurdler combines basic sprint technique with other specialized leg and arm movements to help him through the various phases of his event.

The Sprinter's Arm Action
The elbows remain bent at a right angle and close to the sides, the hands pump as high as the forehead and as far back as behind the waist. The faster a sprinter can move his arms in this manner, the faster he can run.

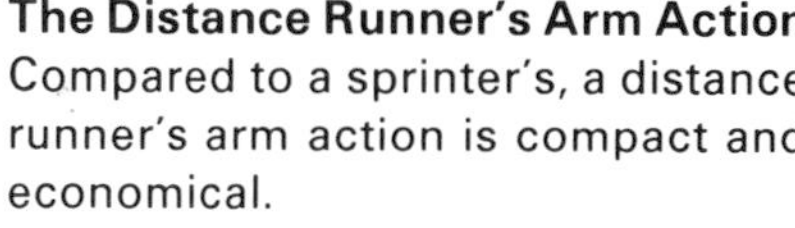

The Distance Runner's Arm Action
Compared to a sprinter's, a distance runner's arm action is compact and economical.

Putting It All Together: The Sprinter

A

B

Perfect sprinting requires perfect form. Here, two-time Olympian Harvey Glance shows the form that helped win him an Olympic gold medal. Harvey's arms form approximately a 90-degree angle at the elbow and serve as pistons to drive the upper body straight ahead. The elbows are kept to the sides and, as the arms pump forward, the hands go no higher than the forehead to avoid dissipating the arms' forward momentum. As the arms pump backward, the hands go no further than the

C

D

hips before they begin their forward thrust. The hips and shoulders, meanwhile, remain level and relaxed through every phase of the sprinting motion, and the knees are bent and lifted high to the level of the hips to allow optimum forward extension of the lower leg. Note Harvey's foot placement—he lands on the toes and the ball of the foot. All his leg and arm actions are directed forward, not sideways, so that his body moves in a straight line.

Putting It All Together: The Distance Runner

A

B

Level hips and shoulders, lower knee and arm lift, and a more relaxed and upright body position than a sprinter's characterize the distance runner's form. Note, too,

C

D

how the arms cross slightly in front of the upper body—a more natural arm swing than the sprinter's powerful pumping motion.

The Middle-Distance and Distance Runner's Arm Action

The by-word for the middle-distance and distance runner is efficiency. His goal is to run as fast, and yet *as steadily* as he can over distances far greater than those run competitively by any sprinter. Thus, he seeks an arm action that quickly *yet comfortably* propels him forward and requires the least expenditure of energy. Most middle-distance runners adopt a kind of modified sprinter's arm action, still swinging the arms from the shoulders, but less vigorously, keeping them more loose and relaxed, and even dropping the hands lower and letting the forearms swing slightly across the body for greater comfort.

Distance runners reduce their arm movement even more to conserve energy, and some, such as the great Finish runner, Lasse Viren, are known to carry their hands close to their bodies and move them slightly across the chest with only minimal shoulder force.

To each his own. If you're a middle-distance or distance runner, you should experiment to find the arm action with which you feel most comfortable. Whichever you choose, you should nevertheless be sure to *keep your shoulders level, not hunched, elbows tucked in and not flapping.* With level shoulders and tucked elbows, the other components of your arm action—arm swing, elbow flexion, hand position, etc.—should fall easily into place.

RUNNING THE CURVE

We teach the athlete—sprinter or distance runner—to swing his right arm across his body slightly, drop his left shoulder and bring his right leg over to help him run the curve more easily.

Running the Curve
To run curves easier, do as this sprinter does: swing your right arm across your body slightly, drop your left shoulder, and bring your right leg over to the left.

Britain's Sebastian Coe displays the form that has made him a middle-distance champion.

RUNNING HILLS

In downhill running, the runner should let his arms drop and let his body relax while he goes as fast as is comfortable, without holding back.

In uphill running, the runner must pump his arms vigorously to negotiate the hill. He should also try to exaggerate his knee lift. At the top of the hill, the runner goes back to his normal stride.

THE SPRINT START: TYPES OF STARTS

If all the sprinters in a race can run the 100 meters in 10.1 seconds, the one with the best start will win. That's why it's important to place a great deal of emphasis on starting techniques. If you're a sprinter, starting well puts you in running position for the rest of the race, no matter what the distance. By contrast, if you stumble out of the blocks or chop your steps, you'll be left behind trying to regain your balance.

As a sprinter, you should concentrate on getting into good sprint position as quickly as possible rather than coming out low. Ideally, you should be in good running position by *your third step!* You can't be running at top speed if you are leaning too much. By changing Harvey Glance's starting technique and teaching him to lean less, we helped him become a world-class sprinter instead of just a good one. Glance had been taught originally to stay low out of the blocks and come up slowly. That's bad technique. You should feel confident, comfortable, powerful, and efficient coming out of the blocks, and you should come up quickly.

Three types of starts are most commonly used in sprinting today. They are the *bunched start,* the *medium start,* and the *elongated start.* Let's look at each.

The Bunch Start

The bunch start places the front foot approximately 18 inches behind the starting line and the back foot about 28 inches behind the line. As a result, the bunch start creates a narrow, tight base from which the sprinter shoots forward. Ideally, the bunch start allows the sprinter to rocket from the blocks, and it should put him ahead at about the 20-meter mark. Many track people, however, including ourselves, question how well the bunch start puts the athlete into good running position for the rest of the race. Many times, the sprinter who uses the bunch start risks stumbling as he comes out of the blocks.

The Elongated Start

This start goes to the other extreme, placing the feet farther apart. The lead foot is about 14 inches behind the line while the back foot is 42 inches behind. Supposedly, this start gives the sprinter a broader base of support, so that when he finally gets to full speed, he will be in better running position for the rest of the race. At 20 meters, however, he will be behind the person using the bunch start if both have the same reactions.

The Medium Start

Though both the bunch start and the elongated start could vary by an inch or two in either direction, the most comfortable start seems to be somewhere in between those extremes. The medium start allows the runner to get out of the blocks quickly enough to be in the race early, yet allows him to adjust to full running speed and position efficiently.

In the medium start, the lead foot is about 14 inches behind the line and the trailing foot is just 20 inches further back. Our athletes have found this to be a very comfortable and yet efficient base of support.

THE SPRINT START: GETTING INTO THE BLOCKS

Let's say you're a sprinter about to run a competitive race. After setting the block at the desired spacing, you should check to make sure that your left block is forward if you are right-handed, and your right block is forward if you are left-handed, to give yourself the most power out of the blocks from your dominant side.

When you hear the starter call "On your marks," you should move from your waiting position, behind the blocks to a point forward of them so that you can back into them. Carefully place your left foot against the block, making sure, in accordance with IAAF, NCAA, and high school rules, that your toes touch the track, then stretch your right foot over the back block, doing a kicking maneuver to get out the kinks, and put the right foot forward in position against the rear block. Again place your toes against the track, and put your right knee on the ground near your left foot.

Your fingers should be placed behind the line, but as close as possible without touching it. Your hands each form a "V," or a tripod with the thumb and four fingers, while the arms are placed just outside the thighs.

This is actually a resting position, since you may often be forced to wait as long as ten to twenty seconds for the other runners to get into position. Make sure your weight is evenly distributed between your hands and feet while you are waiting. In a race situation, you must wait until the starter sees that everyone has become motionless. Only then will he go to the next command.

Whether you are at practice or in a race, you should look down the track about three meters while concentrating on the voice of the starter. On the command, "Set," you should think only of raising your hips into position.

Starting Blocks and Starting Positions
The blocks in the foreground are set for the bunch start, the blocks in the middle for the medium start, and the blocks in the back for the elongated start.

Many sprinters feel that the position for the medium start *(middle)* gives them the most comfortable, yet efficient, starting base.

THE SPRINT START: RUNNERS SET

On the "Set" command, take a breath, hold it, and raise your hips so that your backside is only slightly higher than your head. Holding your breath is done for no other reason than to help you concentrate. Concentration is essential, as the next sound will be the start, sending you from your mark. Normally, you will remain in the set position for about two seconds, but the actual period depends upon the individual starter.

The Sprinter's Start

A

B

The sprinter readies himself for the start with a last-moment leg stretch (A). When the starter says, "Take your marks," the sprinter backs his feet into the blocks (B,C),

C

D

kneels, and places the tips of his thumbs and forefingers as close to the starting line as possible without touching it (D).

The Sprinter's Start (Cont.)

E

At the "Set" command, the sprinter takes a breath and holds it while raising his hips to the starting position (E).

F

At the crack of the starting gun, the sprinter throws his left arm forward as the rear foot leaves the block and blows out the breath of air he's been holding (F). His left leg applies a great deal of force against the front block.

G

H

I

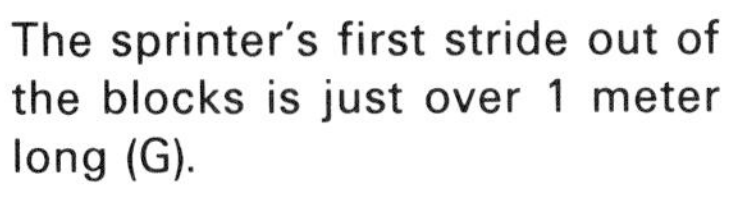

The sprinter's first stride out of the blocks is just over 1 meter long (G).

Subsequent steps are increasingly longer, so that by the fifth or sixth step, the sprinter has come out of his starting crouch and attained proper stride length, normally about 2 meters (H,I).

THE SPRINT START: AT THE GUN

The moment you hear the gun, you should begin a series of explosive actions. Release your left hand, throwing the arm forward as the rear foot leaves the block. Blow out the breath of air you've been holding and begin a breathing pattern you should maintain for the rest of the race and in which you take in as much air as possible. At the same time, lift your right hand off the ground, bring it back, and move your left foot from the block. With this action, your right arm goes forward and your left arm comes back. A great deal of force is applied against the front block, while your back foot releases from the rear block. Your body should start to rise as you drive your arms vigorously, and your head is in natural alignment with your trunk.

Assuming you are of average height (5′8″ to 6′0″), your first stride out of the blocks should be just over one meter, with each step gradually increasing until approximately two meters in length. You should attain your proper stride length by the fifth or sixth stride and should maintain it throughout the race. Again, *your first goals are attaining full running stride and position as soon as possible, not staying low,* contrary to what has often been taught.

As you move down the straightaway, your arms should be swinging vigorously and straight ahead, your knees coming up, the feet touching the ground as described earlier, and legs kicking back toward the buttocks. Your body should lean forward considerably at the start, then become more and more upright throughout the race. *Always keep the body's center of gravity over the lead leg.*

Just as you should strive for relaxation in the actual race, you should also strive for it during the start. Though the start is an explosive action, your ability to relax in the blocks is critical. Remember to cup your hands to avoid tightening up, and start a crisp, economical breathing pattern at a rhythm with which you're comfortable the moment you spring from the blocks.

FALSE STARTS

Never guess on when the starting gun will go off. The days when the 1912 Olympic 100-meter final in Stockholm had seven false starts and no disqualifications are gone forever. Now, almost all forms of competition, except the Olympics, have gone to the "no false start" rule. If a runner jumps the gun, he's out. If a sprinter false-starts in practice, he should be made to run a lap on the track. If the embarrassment isn't enough to make him wait for the sound, it's interesting how quickly he learns to hold at the start to keep from building up the unwanted mileage.

Greg Foster probably lost the 110-meter hurdle race in the 1984 Olympics because he just shaded the gun, or false-started. Foster was so sure they would fire the gun again, to recall the race, that he hesitated and lost his concentration. He knew he shouldn't have, but nonetheless eased up a bit—enough to keep him from winning. Foster did run a great race to recover and get a close second to Roger Kingdom. Still, the basic point remains: To win a race, you must start *at* the sound of the gun, not before it.

THE DISTANCE RUNNER'S START

In races above 800 meters, the runner will use a standing start, as it is only a two-command start: "Take your marks," and the gun. He will have his left foot next to the starting line, his right foot 12 inches back and his right arm in front

The Distance Runner's Start

In races 800 meters or longer, use a standing start and expect to hear only two commands: "Take your marks" and the gun. Place one foot near the starting line, the other, 12 or so inches back. The arm opposite the forward leg should also be forward (A) for maximum starting thrust (B).

A

B

of the line. As the gun goes off, his right foot comes forward and his left hand goes out, uppercutting in good running form. If the runner starts with his other foot forward, all positions are reversed. Even in distance running, good technique on the start can gain valuable distance and get the runner out in good position.

THE FINISH: THE LEAN

No matter whether you are a sprinter or a distance runner, you should always be sure to lean at the finish, regardless of the margin of victory. This is especially important when the photo timer is used. The lean shows up much better in the pictures and may decide the race in your favor or move you up a position or two.

During the 100 meters at the 1932 Olympics in Los Angeles, it appeared that either Thomas "Eddie" Tolan and Ralph Metcalfe of the United States had finished in a dead heat, or that Metcalfe had won. Judges viewed film of the race later and decided that Tolan had crossed the line two inches ahead of Metcalfe. We now go by the rule that the first runner to *reach* the finish line, not *cross* it, is the winner, and that means Metcalfe did indeed win the race.

You lean at the finish by thrusting your chest out and throwing your arms back. Timing is important in the lean, because if you lean at the wrong time, it can cost you the race. Harvey Glance used to have a problem with leaning too early. He leaned too soon in the 1976 Olympic final and wound up fourth in the 100. That was the first time the pressure got to him all season and his whole race fell apart. He got behind, started to overstride, and leaned too soon. Of course, leaning too late also defeats the purpose.

You should lean only at the last stride of your race. Like every other aspect of sprinting, you should practice the lean during the regular training routine. At regular times during workouts, make a point of leaning at the end of every repetition sprint.

The Sprinter's and Distance Runner's Lean at the Finish

As Harvey Glance demonstrates, you lean at the finish by thrusting your chest out and throwing your arms straight back.

Evelyn Ashford timed her lean perfectly in her victory in the 100 meters at the 1984 Olympics in Los Angeles.

THE HIGH HURDLES

The high hurdles is an event that combines running (usually 60 to 110 meters) with a particular skill: jumping over barriers that are anywhere from two feet six inches to three feet six inches high. In years past, coaches often identified the hurdler as the tall, rangy runner who lacked the raw speed of the sprinters, but who could become an asset to the team if he could master hurdling technique.

Over the years that philosophy has changed as faster and faster athletes have learned how to hurdle, and more and more their speed *between* the hurdles has determined who will win. Today's outstanding hurdler has speed, agility, coordination, flexibility, strength, and a bit of courage. The first five traits belong to all skilled athletes, but the last element is that ability to hit the hurdle or the ground and have the pluckiness to go back out and try again.

Hurdling

No matter what height you hurdle, you should apply the following techniques. First, as you approach the hurdle, concentrate on its topmost bar (A, B).

A

B

Beginning to Hurdle

If you're a beginning hurdler, start by setting up three hurdles one foot in height and work on going over them. The hurdles should be spaced eight meters apart for men and seven meters apart for women. Run through this pattern at least four times to get a feel for the rhythm of easy, comfortable hurdling technique, and work on taking three strides between each hurdle.

Once you feel comfortable hurdling at the one-foot height, raise the hurdle to 18 inches, repeat the pattern four times, and concentrate on getting your rear, or trailing, foot flat—that is, the inside of the rear foot parallel to the ground. After you have caught the rhythm of the trail foot, focus your attention on staying balanced while hurdling.

It is important that you feel comfortable and balanced, and that your arms help give you balance in what is known as an opposite arm relationship. What that means is that your lead arm should always be the arm opposite the foot

As your lead foot clears the hurdle, your opposite arm should be forward and pointing down, and the foot of the trail leg should be flat—that is, the inside of the foot should be parallel with the bar (C).

C

On the landing (D), the toes of the lead foot touch the ground, while the opposite arm has been pulled back; then the trail leg comes forward, with the knee high, in preparation for a full stride.

D

that goes over the hurdle. You should try to reach out and swing the lead arm back as the rear foot flattens out. After running through a series of these drills at 18 inches, you should then raise the hurdles to two feet and continue to practice the same skills: back leg flat and lead arm out, then swinging the arm back until the hurdle is cleared. To finish this initial session, raise the hurdles to thirty inches and try going over them six times.

You may have difficulty in that first session going over all the hurdles clearly and successfully, but if you have the courage to come back the next day and try again, you should begin your second session with some concentrated stretching, especially working on the ground in what is known as the hurdler's stretch (see illustrations) and around the hurdle, too. You should then pick up where you left off last time, with the hurdles at 30 inches high and eight meters apart. Once you feel you have the balance and rhythm that you developed in the first session, concentrate on the action of your lead leg as it approaches the hurdle. Your front foot should be thrown *directly at the hurdle, not around it,* with the knee bent slightly so that when the foot hits the ground it can quickly paw the ground and drive the leg forward.

The Hurdler's Ground Stretch
This is a beautiful exercise for developing timing and muscle memory for the hurdles. Here, Olympic hurdler James Walker has sat on the ground in the hurdling position and now pumps his arms as if he were taking three strides toward the hurdle (A,B). At the end of three pumps, he points his lead arm forward exactly as he would when clearing a hurdle (C), and then smoothly sweeps his arm to the side (D,E) to complete the hurdling motion.

A

B

C

The Hurdler's Stretch
This passive stretch is an excellent way to prepare the leg and back muscles for hurdling. Hold the stretch for a maximum of eight seconds.

D

E

Hurdling Form

If you are a right-footed hurdler—that is, if you tend to lead with your right foot—then your right arm, as you hurdle, should be to the side in a running position, elbow bent at a 90-degree angle. At the same time, your left arm should be stretched out in front of the shoulder for balance. (Note: The more you point your left hand downward, the quicker your right, or lead, foot will hit the ground, and the sooner you can move on to the next hurdle.) As your left leg, or trail leg in this instance, comes through, the left arm swings back to maintain balance. Once you hit the ground, you should take three normal strides between hurdles, neither rushing nor stretching to clear them. With the hurdle at 30 inches, make your take-off at approximately 6 feet before the

Hurdling Form

Throughout this sequence, note how James Walker attacks the hurdle. He dives at it, jackknifing his body forward from the waist until it is almost parallel with the thigh of his lead leg. Note also how the shoulders remain squared to the front throughout all the gyrations of the hurdling action. This helps him keep his balance, so important

(A) Walker begins his approach. Eyes on the top bar and running at full speed, he carries his arms high to help him shift his weight forward and lifts his lead leg as he comes up on his toes.

(B) As he pushes off the ground, the lower half of the lead leg begins to pivot up from the knee, adding to the upward and forward momentum. The body leans forward from the waist, and the arm opposite the lead leg is thrust forward and downward from the shoulder.

(C) As the lead leg begins to pass over the hurdle, the trail leg begins to rotate from the hip and the knee starts to swing up and out. Note how Walker keeps his shoulders squared.

hurdle and land about 3 feet beyond the hurdle. As the height is raised to 42 inches, take off about a foot sooner and land a foot later. Repeat this procedure for six hurdles 8 meters apart for ten sets. Again, work on balance and rhythm while maintaining good form.

After you have worked a week in this manner, it's time to move to the high hurdle height at which you will be competing. For high school girls the height is 33 inches; for high school boys, 39 inches; college women, 36 inches; college men, 42 inches. Begin by working with two hurdles 9 meters apart. After several attempts at clearing both, add another hurdle to the series. As the week wears on, work up to six hurdles, and ten to twelve repetitions. Once you can handle this, start on some hurdling drills and begin hurdling at the regular distance of 10 yards apart for men and 26 feet 3 inches for women.

to maintaining sprinting speed while clearing the hurdles. The arm on the side of the lead leg is also used to help him keep his balance.

Notice throughout the sequence how the fingers are loosely clenched or extended, indicating the relaxation of nonessential muscles despite intense concentration on the job of clearing the hurdle.

(D) With the body directly over the hurdle, the lead foot has already begun to descend, dropping below the plane of the top bar. Walker now begins to pull the trail leg over the hurdle; as the knee of the trail leg whips over the hurdle, the toe is turned up and will clear. Walker is already eyeing the top of the next hurdle.

(E) As Walker prepares to land, both of his arms help him keep his balance, while the trail leg is pulled through with the knee very high. High knee lift helps make the next stride long enough to maintain speed between the hurdles and ensure arrival at the correct takeoff point for the next hurdle.

(F) Well into his next stride, Walker reaches out with the trail leg while driving hard off the toes of the lead leg. His arms have reverted to normal sprinting action, and his balance is perfect, resulting in a minimum loss of speed.

Drills for Hurdlers

If you're a beginning hurdler you should work the following three drills into your regular routines. First, space the hurdles 10 yards apart and work on running to the side of the hurdle with five quick steps, clearing the hurdle with your trailing foot only. Concentrate on keeping your back leg flat and the toe pointed out.

Second, work on the other side of the hurdles throwing only your front foot over the hurdle and taking five steps in between.

Last, stand in front of the hurdle, place your lead leg against the top bar, and "paw" at the hurdle (see illustrations). You should do these drills and others like them at the beginning of each hurdle session.

The Trail Leg Drill
By working on clearing the hurdle with your trail leg only, you learn to keep the leg flat and the toe pointed out.

A

B

C

The Lead Foot Drill
This drill, wherein you throw only your lead foot over the bar, teaches the timing and momentum needed for correct clearance.

The Pawing Drill
This drill, wherein you approach the bar slowly, but touch it only with your lead foot, sharpens both hurdling form and timing.

A

B

Hurdles Races

Once you master the basic skills and techniques of hurdling, you're ready to train with some competitive aspects in mind. In competition, the hurdler who can get out of the blocks quickly and in hurdling position will have an edge over his opponent. The key to a successful race is to get over the first hurdle in position for the next nine hurdles. If you start your jump too close to the first hurdle, or if you are off-balance, you lose valuable time as you try to regain your rhythm and balance. If you hit the first hurdle, you will be short coming off the hurdle and will have to reach to get to the next one, again losing valuable tenths of seconds. We recommend that our hurdlers use a medium to elongated start so that they will get out in a higher position and will be running tall through the first hurdle. If you stay too low out of the blocks, you will not be able to get into position to clear the hurdle.

How well athletes clear early hurdles often determines the outcome of the race.

If you compete in the hurdles, you'll soon find that the sprint to the first hurdle often sets the tone for the race. A hurdler tends to be intimidated by a rival ahead of him swinging his arm back as he clears the next hurdle. Different lead-leg hurdlers can hinder, or even hit, each other. The time that you spend practicing your starts out of the blocks will pay off when the season starts.

Always think about your body position as you come over a hurdle, concentrating on a good stretch and lean. If your stretch and lean are correct, you won't catch the hurdles with your back leg. For women, the lean is not quite so pronounced, since they usually have the leg length to clear the lower hurdles. You should practice reaching the first hurdle in eight steps and taking three steps before each subsequent one, knowing that if you take four or five steps, or chop your stride, you will lose precious time between hurdles.

Not only must you be proficient in the technical aspects of hurdling, you must also work on your speed. You must come off the hurdle efficiently, in position to use your speed to reach the next hurdle. If all hurdle technique is equal between hurdles, rhythm and speed will win the race: after the last hurdle, the last 15 meters are a sprint to the finish.

The Intermediate Hurdles

The progression for learning to run the 400-meter intermediate hurdles is the same as for learning the high hurdles. Once you get the hurdle technique down for one leg, however, we recommend that you work on leading with the opposite leg, for two reasons. First, if it works well for your stride, you can take fourteen steps between hurdles and alternate legs at each hurdle, or you can take thirteen or fifteen steps and not alternate, but if you get into trouble—if you hit a hurdle, lose your rhythm, and so on—you'll know how to hurdle with your opposite leg, and therefore not have to chop your steps.

Once you are hurdling well at 30 inches, stay at that height if you are a woman, since it is the competitive height for women's hurdles, and move to 36 inches if you are a man. When you have the form down at that height, set up four hurdles at intermediate hurdle distance, which is 35 meters apart, and run these at three-quarters speed just to get the idea of running at close to 400-meter hurdle pace over a few hurdles. Do this six times and see if you require thirteen, fourteen, or fifteen steps between hurdles. Check your form and see what kind of pattern suits you best. The successful intermediate hurdler can run thirteen steps all the way, alternate which foot clears the hurdle by going fourteen steps all the way, run fifteen steps all the way, or alternate for the first five hurdles by running fourteen steps between, then change to fifteen steps for the last five hurdles. Once you have settled on the most comfortable pattern, then, six times a day for a week, run five hurdles set 35 meters apart—but always after some good stretching exercises. When you have this pattern down, it's time to move to the starting line and work toward the first hurdles. The normal number of steps to the first hurdle is twenty-two or twenty-three, and you may take whichever is more comfortable. After practicing your approach to the first hurdle four times, set up three hurdles and work on clearing them in progression six times to get the feel of alternately running and hurdling. One of the things you and your coach should always study is your form going over the hurdle. In particular, you must avoid hooking on the curve. Hooking means letting your trail leg drop outside and below the hurdle as you go over it on the curve, and hurdlers have been disqualified for doing it, especially in big meets where there are many hurdle inspectors. To avoid hooking, simply go

Edwin Moses displays the form that has made him a champion.

over the *middle* of the hurdle on the curve; if your trail leg hits the hurdle, you're not carrying it high enough, but at least you won't be disqualified.

In addition, your coach should watch to make sure that you aren't losing any momentum by chopping or overstriding as you go into each hurdle.

The great Olympic champion Edwin Moses has an ideal stride for taking thirteen steps between hurdles. While most hurdlers are stretching and reaching to take thirteen strides, Moses, who is over 6 feet tall, takes his thirteen steps and the hurdle in stride. Once you learn the race, you'll discover that you more than likely run the intermediate hurdles four seconds slower than you run a flat 400 meters, and as you become more proficient as a hurdler, the time difference will be closer to three seconds. For Moses, the difference is closer to two seconds.

THE STEEPLECHASE

The technique for clearing the hurdles in the steeplechase, a 3,000-meter race around a 400-meter track with four barriers including a water jump, is similar to the technique used in the intermediate hurdles, since the hurdle and barrier are the same height, three feet. The only difference in clearing the barriers in a steeplechase is that you must give yourself a clear shot or position at them —they are fixed in the ground and if you hit them with a foot or leg, you fall; they don't. You should also quicken your stride a little as you move toward the barrier. If you are not a good hurdler, you can, by the rules of the race, step on top of the hurdle and push off—something most steeplechasers do on the water jump barrier. When you step on a steeplechase barrier, your arms should be held out a little for balance, and, as soon as your opposite foot lands beyond the water or in the shallow part of the water, it should absorb the shock of the jump and your other foot should swing out into full running stride. Your arms should then move back into regular position for good running action.

Some successful steeplechasers have been experimenting with hurdling the water jump, rather than stepping on it, to save time. That may be the technique of the future for steeplechasers, but it requires exceptional hurdling ability. If you're new to the steeplechase, you should step *on* the barrier at the water hazard. Remember, once you do so, to jump *forward* more than up, and work at trying to clear the water if possible, since running in waterlogged shoes is fatiguing. More than anything, your height and jumping ability will determine your plan of attack.

Hurdling a Steeplechase Barrier

D

C

The technique for hurdling a steeplechase barrier is the same one used in the intermediate hurdles. The runner quickens his pace as he approaches the barrier (A). As he hurdles it, the arm opposite his lead leg points forward and down to aid in a more efficient hurdling trajectory (B). At the peak of the hurdle, the runner's lead arm

Hurdling a Steeplechase Water Barrier

When clearing the water barrier, do as these world-class steeplechasers: step up on the barrier, spreading your arms for greater stability, and jump forward, not up or down (A).

A

B

A

swings sideways and back for stability while his trail leg pivots up and sideways, the foot parallel with the barrier to clear it (C). On landing, the knee of the trail leg is up and forward for a full stride, and the arms are already in proper running position (D).

B

Keep your arms spread for stability as you land, but once you touch the edge of the water hazard, stride forward, with knees high, to reestablish normal running form quickly (B). Your height and jumping ability will determine where you land.

USA

Strength

Since strength develops power, which, for our purposes we'll define as "explosive strength" or "strength with speed," a weight training program is essential if you're a serious track athlete. Done properly, weight training can help you develop power, aerobic strength, resistance to injury and, to some extent, speed. At Auburn we have found that the key to our strength program is the *consistency* with which our athletes train. Indeed, strength training is so important to us that at the 1977 World University Games in Sofia, Bulgaria, Harvey Glance and I looked all over trying to find a weight room where he could work out since we felt it was important to keep up his strength.

During the fall, or off-season, we have strength sessions every Monday, Wednesday, and Friday for everybody except the cross-country runners. Everybody does basically the same lifts to develop strength. Our fall workout is an overall body conditioning workout, focusing on the legs and upper body. To help motivate our athletes, we include weight tests in their strength program after four and eight weeks. The weight test consists of three separate maximum lifts in the bench press, the military press, and the curl. A runner is allowed three tries in each and counts the one that

In 1980, Willie Smith was the fastest 400-meter man in the world, in part because of the strength training program that he followed.

is best. Let's say, for example, that he starts the test lifting 85 pounds in the curl. If he achieves that, he might then try 95 pounds. If he lifts 95, he has one more try, so he might go for 105. If he fails at 95, say, he must try 95 again. If he still fails, he's given credit for lifting 85 pounds.

If you decide to give yourself a weight test, you arrive at the starting weight according to how much you have been lifting during regular practice sessions.

During the indoor and outdoor track seasons when we have meets on Friday and Saturday, we lift twice a week, Monday and Wednesday. These workouts help our runners maintain their strength and power and still give the muscles enough time to recover by competition day.

During the fall, our cross-country team does weight training on Monday and Wednesday. They do only upper-body work, not to develop strength, but, again, to maintain strength, because it is important that they run well in their meets. (Total-body strength development can slow a runner while his body adapts to any newly minted strength or power.)

To institute a sound weight program, you should first be familiar with basic anatomy and physiology. One of the mistakes often made in strength training is that the program is incomplete—it doesn't work all the major muscle groups, and it fails to exercise muscle groups in opposition to each other. For example, if you do leg extensions to work the quadriceps muscles in the front of your thighs, you must also be sure to work the hamstrings, which work in opposition to the quadriceps, with leg curls. By doing so, you prevent, and in some cases take care of, a muscular imbalance. Quite often, track athletes with a chronic problem of hamstring pulls discover that it is the result of a strength imbalance between the hamstrings and the quadriceps. A basic working knowledge of anatomy relative to strength training is vital to any track athlete's well-being.

As with all successful strength programs, the exercises and lifts should be geared to meet the needs of each individual and by and large should be specific to the athlete's event. A lift that many coaches recommend, the squat, is not one that we do at Auburn because we have found it to be dangerous, especially when done by inexperienced lifters. Squats can lead to back strain, and the gains that the exercise can provide are offset by the loss of training time to injury.

To make our strength program effective and successful, we have adopted the concept of "periodization" or "phase weight training." By periodization we mean breaking the training cycle into four different periods, or phases. These four-period variations in training are day to day (as opposed to month to month, or season to season). We have found that this approach gives our athletes the best of everything in strength training—strength, power, and improved performances in their events.

Leg Extensions and Hamstring Curls

A

B

If you do leg extensions to develop your quadriceps *(above),* you must also be sure to do hamstring curls *(below)* to strengthen the opposing muscles and avoid muscular imbalance.

The periodization concept in weight training is very similar to the philosophy most coaches use in training distance runners, and for the track athlete consists of four phases. In the first phase, the *hypertrophy phase,* the athlete develops muscle bulk and generally builds a sound base of strength from which he can develop further. Phase two is the *basic strength phase;* phase three, the *strength/power phase;* and phase four, the *maintenance phase.* As you'll see when you study the program, it goes from general to specific strength training: from high-volume/low-intensity workouts at the beginning of the year to low-volume/high-intensity workouts during the championship time of the year.

At Auburn, we do not try to peak in our overall training for a certain meet, but rather we try to run fast and improve every week we race. We feel that periodization can help any track athlete maintain and improve strength over a long competitive season without the work becoming dull or boring.

Basic Strength Exercises

The Bench Press
With a spotter standing behind you, lie flat on a weight bench, with your feet flat on the floor. Grasp the bar with your hands slightly wider apart than a shoulder's width apart (A).

After exhaling, take the bar off the rack and slowly lower it to your chest, inhaling through the entire movement (B).

A

B

The Bicep Curl
Holding a bar below your waist with your hands facing outwards (A), slowly curl the bar to your chest (B). Lower the bar slowly and repeat. The bicep curl strengthens the wrist, forearm, and biceps muscles—all critical to proper running form.

Once the bar touches your chest (C), raise it slowly, exhaling as you do so, until your arms are straight again. Repeat. The bench press strengthens the muscles of the chest, upper arms, shoulders, and upper back, and it also stretches the rib cage. Variations of the bench press can be done with the bench at a 45-degree incline or with the hands closer or farther apart.

Single Arm Curls
Curls can also be done with dumbbells *(left)* or weight plates *(right)*. Sprinters often do single arm curls quickly to duplicate the explosive arm movement of sprinting.

Sit-ups
The bent-knee sit-up remains one of the best means for strengthening the abdominal muscles. Adding a twisting movement to the sit-up works the oblique (outside) abdominal muscles.

A

B

The Seated Military Press
Seated at the edge of a bench, with the hands holding the bar at chest level and a shoulder's width apart (A), push the bar straight up until the arms are locked overhead (B). Lower the bar slowly and repeat. This exercise, which can also be done standing, generally exercises the large muscles of the upper body. To work the muscles of the neck and back further, start and finish the seated press with the bar behind the neck.

The Bent-Arm Pullover
This exercise, performed here on a Nautilus machine, works the latissumus dorsi muscles located on the outside of the back, the triceps muscles in the upper arm, the pectoral or chest muscles, and the deltoids of the upper back. You can also do pullovers with a straight arm to work the serratus muscles of the underarm, and either type can be done using free weights and a bench. Simply lie on the bench as you would for a bench press, extend your hands behind you, and have a spotter hand you the bar. With arms bent or straight, slowly lift the bar over your head to your chest. Lower. Repeat.

A

B

A

B

The Lat Pulldown

This exercise, which works the latissimus dorsi muscles of the back, requires a weight stack attached to a pulley/handle system. Seated or kneeling, grasp the handle and slowly draw it toward your chest, a few inches below your chin. Raise the handle slowly and repeat. You can also do lat pulldowns with your hands close together or with your body facing away from the weight stack and the handle pulled behind your neck.

Toe Raises

With a weighted bar held comfortably behind the neck, place the balls of the feet on a platform two to three inches above floor level and slowly rise up on the toes (as shown). Toe raises are an excellent way to strengthen the calf muscles and should be a regular part of a sprinter's weight program.

A

B

Dips
This exercise, which works the triceps, pectoral (chest), and front deltoid (shoulder) muscles, requires either a dipping bar (found in most gyms) or a set of parallel bars used by gymnasts.

Back Hyperextensions
Also known as back-ups, back hyperextensions strengthen the muscles of the lower back, so often vulnerable to pain and injury from running. Note the position of the body (B)—only slightly beyond parallel with the ground.

A

B

A

B

Erect Rows

This exercise works the triceps muscles as well as most of the muscles of the shoulders and upper back. From the starting position (A), pull the barbell upward (B),

C

D

moving your elbows laterally rather than backwards. As you continue to raise the bar, keep it close to your body (C). At the finish, the bar should almost touch the chin (D). Now slowly lower the bar to the starting position.

PHASE ONE: HYPERTROPHY

Phase I, the hypertrophy phase, when the muscles get bigger, lasts three weeks and generally should take place when the runner is not competing. If you decide to follow this program, as a rule, you should perform three sets of ten repetitions for each lift. We recommend doing exercises that will benefit your overall strength and conditioning—that is, the exercises taken together exercise all the body's major muscle groups—and that are simple to do. Some sample lifts for different athletes in Phase I are as follows:

3 × 10

bench press	leg extension
incline bench press	behind neck press (seated)
curls	leg curls
abdominal work	super pullovers
military press	lat pulls

Taken together, these exercises work all the major muscle groups and, done over a period of three weeks, three days a week, will help you build a sound base for further strength work.

PHASE TWO: BASIC STRENGTH

The second phase of the strength program is the basic strength period. In it, you raise the weight (load) you lift and reduce the repetitions (volume) to eight per set of exercises. This phase of the program also lasts three weeks. Some more exercise examples:

3 × 8

bench press	erect row
incline press	leg extension
curls	leg curls
abdominal work	toe raises
roman chair (back hyperextensions)	military press

PHASE THREE: STRENGTH/POWER

The third phase, or strength/power phase of the program, shifts its focus from high-volume/low-intensity to low-volume/high-intensity training to develop strength *and* power. It is kind of a transition phase and again lasts only three weeks. By then, you should be into or approaching your regular season, when good power is a necessity. In this phase, it helps to have your work monitored by a strength coach because the weight that you now lift increases dramatically to as much as 95 percent of your personal best in any given lift, and to receive full benefit from the phase, you must be certain that every lift you do is technically correct. A good mix of lifts could include:

3 × 5

bench press (using dumbbells)	abdominal work
leg curls	roman chair (back hyperextensions)
leg extensions	military press
curls (using dumbbells)	dips (with extra weight, using vest, belt, etc.)
pullovers (prone on bench)	toe raises

PHASE FOUR: MAINTENANCE

The fourth, or maintenance, phase, is a low-volume/high-intensity period that can last the remainder of the season. By then you should be in excellent condition. To stay that way, your time in the weight room should be kept to a minimum. The number of repetitions is now down to three per set of three, two days a week. The amount of weight should be as close to maximum as possible while maintaining correct technique for nine repetitions. You must try not to get stale mentally, as this last phase runs the entire duration of your competitive season.

3 × 3

Use the same exercises as before, but change them periodically to avoid boredom.

Strength and power, along with speed, make winners out of runners.

WEIGHT TESTS

These help motivate our athletes in the fall or off-season, and are given after four and eight weeks. Each athlete weighs in before the test and is placed in a weight group, such as 140 and below, 140–149, or 150–159. Records are kept on a large board in the weight room listing the athlete and his weight division, lifts, total, and year. Our athletes have goals to work for (see page 107), and when we record the results we note in plus or minus poundage whether the athlete has improved or not from year to year and from test to test. This helps make the strength program an important part of the fall program and keeps the competitive juices flowing.

POST-SEASON

After the competitive season it's essential that you take some time off from weight training. One or possibly two weeks of active rest or some other type of activity—tennis, basketball, hiking, biking, swimming, etc.—is a welcome break that gives your body time to recover after six to nine months of running and weight lifting. After the active rest period, you can begin the periodization process starting at the hypertrophy phase, and continuing through all the others, but on a higher plane of achievement than the year before.

721
271
576
695
622
385

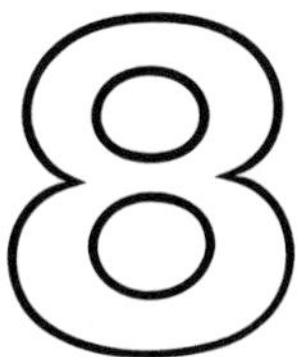

Tactics

Strange as it may seem, when you run competitively, you do not simply get in the blocks, leave when the gun goes off, and win for dear old Auburn. You have to have a race plan, a strategy.

Race strategy cannot be decided on the spur of the moment when the starter says, "On your marks." Long in advance, whether you are running short sprints or a marathon, you need a plan of action to tell you when to make a move or when to let others direct the flow of the race.

Some basic preparation is so simple that people actually forget to carry it out, such as remembering to bring your shoes to the track. Other strategy is complex, such as being prepared to alter your tactics according to the other runners in the field so that you aren't stuck with an inappropriate plan if the race doesn't go as you expected.

Let's go through each race, from the 100 meters to the marathon, focusing on critical points in each that require a plan. First, however, there's the lull before the gun.

Strategy is a complex matter and varies according to the field.

PRE-RACE TACTICS

When you step onto the track, you should first check your equipment, make sure your shoes are tied, your shirt tucked into your shorts, and your number on your back or front. You have finished your warmup* by now, and if you are a sprinter, you set up your blocks, making sure they are firmly fixed, and then you take a practice start in your sweats. Okay, now sit down behind your blocks, or if you are a distance runner, take a few strides in your lane. When the starter tells you to pull off your sweats, do so and neatly put them in the basket that is provided by the race organization. Always fold your sweats carefully; take your time: being meticulous and neat shows confidence.

You can also exude confidence in another manner. As you return to the track, confidently shake hands with your nearest competitors and then stand behind your blocks and think through the race: how you will react to the gun, come out of the blocks driving hard, get into stride, move your legs and arms, look straight ahead, and drive all the way to the finish line.

PSYCHING UP AND PSYCHING OUT

Psyching up is a feeling, and a look, of confidence. Charlie Paddock, who won the 100 meters at the Olympics in 1920, used to knock on "a friendly piece of wood" on his way to the starting line. Some sprinters try to psych people out by being the last ones in the blocks or the last ones to take their sweats off. Others shake hands with everybody, wishing them luck by looking them in the eye as if to say, "I've already got you beaten."

Whenever the 400 meters race was mentioned during the 1984 Olympics, you heard that Bert Cameron of Jamaica had the gold medal in his pocket with his name on it, Antonio McKay of the United States was going to break the world record, Innocent Egbunike of Nigeria had already beaten all of the others and expected to win, Sunder Nix of the U.S. team runs well in the big meets and should be a factor, and Darren Clark of Australia had run three good races and might surprise people. Another U.S. runner, however, Alonzo Babers, told the press that Cameron sure looked good in the semifinals, McKay was a real talent, and he, Babers, was just thrilled to get into the finals. The gold medal

---

*The warmup for the sprinter should consist of two easy laps around the track, ten minutes of stretching, and three or four wind sprints. The distance runner should do four to six easy laps, ten minutes of stretching, and three to four wind sprints. These warmup routines should be followed precisely for every competition.

The Victor as Underdog
Alonzo Babers *(center)* surprised everyone—except himself—when he won the men's 400 meters in the 1984 Olympic Games.

wound up around Babers' neck, as he won in 44.28, the fastest 400 meters in 1984. McKay was third and Cameron didn't run because of an injury he suffered in the semis. What do we learn from this? *That you should never give your opponents, particularly if they are underdogs, something to inspire them.* Also, that it's easier to talk after you win than to explain why you lost.

Another example of too much talk involved Auburn's first great sprinter, Clifford Outlin, who in 1974 went to the Soviet Union to compete in the 60-meter dash. He roomed with Mike McFarland, who kept telling Outlin how he, McFarland, would win the 60 and set a record, how he would show the Russians, and so forth. McFarland talked the whole week. Outlin listened but didn't say much. On the day of the race, as they warmed up and took off their USA sweats, Outlin went up to McFarland and said quietly, "I've been listening to you talk all week. Now it's time to go, and I'm going to blow your doors." He did, and in fact Outlin's 6.4 tied the world record. Again, don't get your opponent excited!

To us, the best psych is winning your qualifying heat and winning it in a fast time. A lot of runners try to win their heats easy, coasting across the finish line while looking around to see if anyone is gaining on them. Aren't they surprised when they see that someone is! Others barely qualify for the next round, not minding if someone passes them and knocks them back to, say, third, the last qualifying spot.

From our experience, we think that both winning a heat and running it in a good time show the others that you are ready. Running all races hard and relaxed also leads to a consistent level of intensity.

Great Britain's Sebastian Coe, the 1980 and 1984 gold medalist in the 1,500 meters, likes to psych out his competitors by slowing down at the finish as if to show he could have run faster and won easily. This is a dangerous ploy that doesn't always work.

Alberto Juantorena, for example, the 1976 Olympic gold medalist in the 400 and 800 meters, was competing in the 800 in the 1983 World Championships in Helsinki. In the semifinals, the Cuban was running well, and, to show he had the race won, slowed down to a jog and looked over his shoulder. The next thing Juantorena knew, he stepped on the curb and broke his foot. That's why that psych is dangerous.

By easing up on his way to the finish in the 800 meters semifinals during the 1983 World Championships in Helsinki, Alberto Juantorena broke his concentration—and his foot.

When you're 30 meters from finishing, *it makes no sense to ease up.* You should continue to run hard right through to the end and win your heat. There's no use conserving energy, if it means that by saving your best, the next day you're sitting in the stands next to your coach. Always run your best. Don't get arrogant. Don't get cute.

LANE ASSIGNMENT

The luck of the draw can do more to psych out an athlete than the tactics of a dozen of his opponents. In the 400 especially, a particular lane assignment can fill a sprinter with dread or make him feel as if he's in control—when he hasn't yet set foot on the track. Before the advent of all-weather tracks in the 1960s, the inside lane could be practically destroyed by overuse or by rain. The stigma of drawing Lane One remains. Lane Eight is also feared, while Lanes Four and Five, comfortably in the middle, are the choice assignments. The advantage of drawing one of these middle lanes is that you can see all your opponents much better. By contrast, if you are in Lane One or Lane Eight, you might think that you are winning, only to find in the end that the athlete in the lane farthest from you was the first to cross the line.

Sometimes lanes are given out according to performance in the previous round, the runners with the fastest times being placed in the middle and the others fanned out from them, but in some major meets the athletes draw lots.

The 400 has a staggered start: the runner in Lane One starts at the actual starting line, the runner in Lane Two an additional 23 feet down the track, and so on, all runners remaining in their lanes through the entire race. As such, the runner in Lane One is at a psychological disadvantage because he feels he is always catching up. In fact, by nature of the lane assignments, he won't draw alongside his competitors until the final straightaway. The runner in Lane One also has to run a tighter curve, and that scares runners who are bad at running curves. Lane Eight's drawback is exactly the opposite. Because the runner is so far ahead, he can't see any of the other runners until they either pass him or reach the final 100. Still, many of the great races have been run out of Lane Eight because the runner doesn't have to run as sharp a curve. In fact, he runs a half-curve less—the first curve—and always with the useful fear of knowing that everyone else is, in effect, chasing him.

Your best tactic if you draw either the innermost or the outermost lane is to stay calm and run your own race without measuring your progress against anyone else. In the 1976 Olympic 400-meter hurdles, John Akii-Bua of Uganda

The Staggered Start
Runners in the inner and outer lanes face the biggest tactical disadvantage in a staggered-start race.

was "scared to death," he said, over drawing Lane One. "When you are in Lane One," he said, "you are always the loser. I couldn't sleep that night." Presumably, David Hemery of Great Britain could sleep that night, because he had a better lane and passed the 200-meter mark in 22.8 seconds. The next thing he knew, Akii-Bua was alongside him, and the Ugandan won in a world record time of 47.82. So much for the inside-lane jitters.

STRATEGY: THE 100 METERS

In the short sprints, the 60 indoors and the 100 outdoors, you should want to get out first, but if you don't succeed, you must still keep your form and not press as you try to catch up. Run hard, but *always keep your form,* no matter how tired you feel. As the finish line approaches, prepare yourself to lean, since leaning can often mean the difference between first place and second, or third.

STRATEGY: THE 200 METERS

When running the 200, try to come out of the blocks hard to get around the curve and then float (don't press) for 10 meters on the curve before going into your final sprint. Always lean to the left on the curve, keeping your form all the way down the track, and try to hug the inside of the lane. Ideally, you should lead from the blocks to the finish, but if you break behind, you must catch up and maintain form. Tying up, that is, causing your muscles to tighten and your form to deteriorate from trying too hard, is the bugaboo of sprinters.

Strategy: The 200 Meters
Floating around the curve, as Carl Lewis does here, is a critical strategic element when running the 200 meters.

STRATEGY: THE 400 METERS

In the 400, the strategy is to drive out of the blocks and come through the first 200 meters two seconds faster than the second 200. If you wish to run a 50-second 400, your first 200 should be 24 flat, and your second 200 should be 26 flat. Try to float down the backstretch and pick up a little in the third 100, where the tendency of most runners is to ease up. Coming off the curve, you must pick up the pace—so will everyone else in the race—and your last all-out sprint starts 60 meters from the finish. Be sure to pump your arms hard and try to keep your stride as long as possible without overstriding or shortening up. If you choose not to be the front runner—and most 400 runners don't—your strategy should be to keep within striking distance of your closest opponent, but then again, run your own race so that all your energy is expended when you hit the finish line.

STRATEGY: THE 110-METER HIGH HURDLES

In the high hurdles, the strategy is to get a good start and get to the first hurdle in good position, then keep running hard but comfortably on each hurdle. If you check to see where the opposition is, there's a good chance you'll hit the hurdle, so *you must concentrate only on your own race.* If you do hit a hurdle, it will throw off your stride to the next one. Maintain your cool and lengthen your stride to get back into rhythm.

STRATEGY: THE 400-METER INTERMEDIATE HURDLES

In the intermediate hurdles, you must set a pace, running the race as you would the 400. The first 200 should be two seconds faster than the second 200, and again, you must worry only about your own race. If you see the opposition moving ahead of you and you try to run faster, you'll only throw off your stride and fatigue yourself too soon. You must run at the pattern of thirteen, fourteen, or fifteen steps, or a combination of each, that you set before the race. If the wind is blowing hard, adjust your stride plan: more steps between hurdles going into the wind, less steps with the wind.

STRATEGY: MIDDLE-DISTANCE AND DISTANCE RACES

The best way to run a middle-distance or distance race, from the 800 to the 10,000 meters, is to run each segment at the same pace, running only the first 100 meters and the last hundred meters a little faster. You run the first 100 meters quicker to get position and the last 100 quicker because all athletes try to finish at a sprint. The other parts are run at the same pace to expend your energy evenly. If you wanted to run a four-minute 1,600 meters, for example, the best approach would be to run 59 seconds for the first lap, 61 seconds each for laps two and three, and 59 seconds for the final, or gun, lap. You should

Strategy: The Middle Distances
Timing and position are everything in a middle-distance race. Sebastian Coe, here number 359, eventually broke past the leader to win this 1,500-meter race.

not run anything harder, say, 56, 64, 64, 56. In fact, you couldn't run 56 seconds in the last 400 meters because the 56 in the first 400 would take too much out of you. If you wanted to run a five-minute 1,600-meter race, the best approach, again, is to try to shave only two seconds off the first and last laps for a 74, 76, 76, 74 pace.

Other factors to consider in the race plan are your fastest time and your condition going into the competition. If your fastest time in the 1,600 is 5 minutes, and you are in peak condition, you should set your pace for 4:54, making your two previous fast laps—74 seconds—the new slow ones, give or take a half-second each. You would certainly not set your time for 4:40, as you have never run four laps together at 70 seconds each, and, if you apply the two-second formula—69, 71, 71, 69—the 69-second first lap might take the sting out of you. As a distance runner, then, you must know your capabilities and not look for miracles.

STRATEGY: THE STEEPLECHASE

Steeplechase strategy is the same as in any distance race, that is, you must run according to your own pre-planned pace. But it is not a bad idea to lead so that you can get a clear shot at each barrier. If you are running behind other runners, maneuver to be in position to clear each barrier in stride.

STRATEGY: ROAD RACES AND MARATHONS

The tactics for these races are very simple. First of all, you have to have the courage to run the distance at a pace you can handle. If you run too fast, you'll break down near the end of the race. Usually, in the marathon, this breakdown occurs at the 20-mile mark, which veterans of the race refer to as "The Wall." If you run too slowly, you will get too far behind the leaders and find it difficult to make up ground. You should try to run each mile at an even pace, according to your ability. In other words, you should figure out the final time you are shooting for and divide it by the number of miles in the race. For many athletes, however, contact—that is, being near the top competitors—is necessary, so they must run a little beyond their preferred pace to stay close to the leaders.

If it is a windy day, your strategy should be to run in front when the wind is at your back, and tuck in behind someone when the wind is in your face. That

Strategy: The Marathon
When running a marathon, you should try to run every mile at an even pace, according to your ability.

way, the person in front of you serves as a windshield, and you're less fatigued as the race progresses.

The above are tactics for the star. If you're a competitive jogger, we definitely recommend that you run at a set pace, a little bit faster than your lifetime personal best and taking into account your condition and the weather conditions. If your personal best is a 3-hour marathon, you should strive for 2:55; if 3:30, then strive for 3:20, distributing the time evenly over the entire course of the race. Once again, don't set unrealistic goals for yourself lest you overextend yourself and break down.

For any road race, know where the water stops are and take advantage of them and the sprinklers. Soggy shoes and a wet singlet are far more tolerable than heat prostration and dehydration.

TO LEAD OR TO FOLLOW?

In middle-distance or distance races, if you are running with people of your ability, you must decide if you like to lead or follow. By leading you run at your own pace, you don't have to cut your stride, and you control the tempo. By following, you can watch the field and surprise it with a kick, though you may have to chop your stride to stay behind the leader.

There have been outstanding middle-distance runners who are adept at the different strategies. Joaquim Cruz, Sebastian Coe, Earl Jones, and Mary Decker Slaney are leaders. Steve Ovett, James Robinson, and Don Paige are followers.

On windy days, it is best to be a follower so the leader shields you from the wind. Indoors, it is best to be the leader, running the inside lane to make the followers run wider on the turns. In both instances a predetermined strategy plays its part.

Filbert Bayi took the lead immediately in the 1980 3,000-meter steeplechase event at the Olympics, but his strategy wasn't quite sound. He led by 35 meters with two laps to go, but then he started to tire and was caught on the backstretch by Bronislaw Malinowski of Poland. Why did Bayi, who finished second, try to run so fast so quickly? "Because it's fun," he said, "to run as fast as you can until you are dead-tired." Fine enough, but if Bayi had thought through his race strategy more carefully, he could probably have wound up dead-tired but wearing the gold.

SURGING

This is a strategy whereby the runner runs at a steady pace, then throws in a much faster 200 before going back to a steady pace. Surging is very fatiguing. The person who surges has to have trained to do that. But if you are trained to surge, then anyone who tries to keep up with you will probably fold, or he and everyone else in the race may let you go and lose contact, eventually losing the race. In the 1984 Olympic marathon, Joan Benoit put in one surge and the race was hers.

Kip Keino of Kenya tried to neutralize U.S. star Jim Ryun's kick in the 1968 Olympics 1,500 meters in Mexico City by building up a tremendous lead. Keino had already jogged a mile that day when he got caught in a traffic jam on his way to the stadium, but that was nothing compared to his pace in the

1,500 final. Ben Jipcho, a fellow Kenyan, set a blistering pace of 56 flat for the first lap, but then Keino took the lead and began to pull away. He passed the 800-meter mark in 1:55.3, a killing pace. While the rest of the pack waited for Keino to run out of gas, or even drop out with a gall bladder infection as he had several days earlier in the 10,000, Keino continued to surge. With his finishing kick, Ryun finally did close to within 12 meters of Keino but then fell back. Keino won by 20 meters, the largest margin of victory in Olympic 1,500 history, and set an Olympic record of 3:34.9.

In the 1960 Olympics in Rome, Murray Halberg of New Zealand and his coach, Arthur Lydiard, came up with a plan to win the 5,000 meters. With three laps left, at a time when most runners are gathering strength for their kick on the last lap, Halberg began to sprint. He confused his opponents, who were wondering what had gotten into him, and Halberg ran the tenth lap in 61.1 seconds to build up a 25-meter lead. He ran the next lap as fast as he could, too, but he was exhausting himself with one lap to go. Hans Grodotzki of East Germany gradually closed in, but Halberg held on to win by 8 meters. He then collapsed on his back in the infield. "I had always imagined an Olympic champion was something more than a mere mortal, in fact, a god," Halberg said in his autobiography, *A Clean Pair of Heels.* "Now I knew he was just a human being."

RABBITS

The rabbit is a runner who sets the pace in middle-distance and distance runs so that outstanding people in the race will not have the pressure of setting the pace. The rabbit, who is in the race to help another runner set a world or meet record, is now legal in competition. A good rabbit sets the pace a little bit faster than world record pace for at least the first half of the race.

If the rabbit sets the pace too fast, he does not help the best runners, who will more than likely burn out with him, and if he sets the pace too slow, no records will be broken, so he has to know what he is doing.

Once Tom Byers was a rabbit in a 1,500-meter race and got so far ahead that he realized all he had to do was practically jog in and he would win the race. He stayed with it and won, to the amazement of the spectators and the other runners.

Byers' race is the exception; in most cases, the rabbit is not a viable candidate to win the race and he usually drops out when half or three-quarters of the race is over.

PASSING ON THE TRACK

Normally you should not pass on the inside. A rule of thumb is to pass on the right when you are one stride or more ahead. If you have enough room, however, you can pass on the inside, but if you make contact with another runner, you might be disqualified. Why get yourself in that position? If you do wind up boxed in, keep your cool. You mustn't force your way out of the box.

At the 1984 Olympics, a most unfortunate occurrence marred the women's 3,000-meter run, the infamous Mary Decker–Zola Budd collision. Both runners were accustomed to leading their races, and neither had experience running in a pack. The American, Decker (now Decker Slaney), took the lead for four laps, but on the fifth lap Budd, running for Great Britain, picked up the pace and moved in front of her. Budd was a meter ahead, or at least one stride, but she didn't cut in. Instead, she ran on the outside of Lane One. Decker then decided to run a little faster and regain the lead. She brushed up against Budd's leg, and nothing happened. A few meters later, however, she hit Budd's foot (some say Budd's foot hit her) and she fell down on the track infield. All she could do was watch as the other runners left her behind. Seeing Decker was down, Budd was crushed. Decker had been her idol. As the crowd in Los Angeles booed her, Budd lost her appetite for the race and Maricica Puica of Rumania won the race. That could be tomorrow's trivia question.

Who was at fault? Some will say Mary Decker, others will say Zola Budd, but the lesson to be learned is clear: *you can't move past someone when there is no room.* You must run in the natural box set up until an opening occurs, and then you must expend extra energy to make your bid to get through. Decker had three laps to go, so she had time to wait for her chance to make a move. Sometimes, being boxed in can turn into a tactical advantage. If the race is run at a normal pace, the leader will run a little faster if she feels someone is challenging her to keep the follower in her same position and maintain the lead.

A final note on the Decker–Budd controversy is that no one was disqualified. If Budd had been disqualified, the race probably wouldn't have been rerun with the schedule as tight as it was. Decker couldn't have come back anyway because of the hip injury she sustained in the fall, and that brings up this point: fouls in track are tough on those fouled, more so than in any other sport. The victims gain from the foul in other sports, such as a five-yard penalty in football, a free throw in basketball, and the offender's removal from the game in hockey.

Passing on the Track

Who was at fault in the Decker–Budd collision? No one can say for sure. But the lessons from the race—on passing and cutting in—will be remembered as long as races are run.

A

B

No matter whether he chooses to lead or to follow during a race, Sebastian Coe knows never to be predictable.

In track, if the fouler is disqualified during a final, race officials can order the race to be rerun, minus the disqualified runner. In Decker's case, if Budd had been disqualified, the rule would not have helped her; Decker was injured, and could not have run the race again anyway.

DRASTIC MEASURES

In the 10,000-meter run at the 1979 Pan American Games in Puerto Rico, Herb Lindsay of the United States led for the first twelve laps and then decided to let someone else lead by slowing the pace up considerably. But no one would take the lead. Lindsay unexpectedly ran to the outside of the fifth lane and just stopped. The three runners behind him all ran into each other, but, fortunately for them, didn't fall. They did take the lead and the race continued. This is a dangerous and drastic tactic, and it wasn't as successful as Lindsay had hoped. He finished second.

Another drastic measure occurred at the Drake Relays a few years ago. An Illinois runner was leading with an Oklahoma State runner on his shoulder in the mile leg of the distance medley relay. The Illinois runner suddenly fell to the inside of the track, holding his right thigh, and the Oklahoma State runner moved into the lead. Then to the Oklahoma State runner's surprise, the Illinois runner was suddenly on his shoulder, running right along with him. Another strange move, but this one was successful.

These examples prove that you should learn to run both from the front and from the rear so that your opponents will never typecast you and won't know how to run against you. Although Sebastian Coe usually prefers to lead, sometimes he'll run from the rear just to shake the other runners up. His strategy depends on the other runners in the race and whether he feels he can go for a world record. The bigger the field, the more inclined he is to run from the front so he will have good position. Either way, Coe knows the key: Don't be predictable.

AUS
139
CAN

Relays

Relays are an important part of a track program because most dual meets or large track meets, including the Olympic Games, have two relays—the 4 × 100 meter and the 4 × 400 meter, for both men and women—and the outcome of either can decide an entire meet. Relay carnivals have many more relays, including distance medleys and shuttle hurdle relays, but whatever their number, relays are an excellent opportunity for a team to show its teamwork.

The key to a successful relay is good baton-passing, where both athletes run at the same speed and make full arm extension at the moment of exchange. If the incoming man is running at full speed, the outgoing man leaves at full speed. If the incoming runner comes in on his knees and elbows, then the outgoing runner must go out on his knees and elbows, too. A full arm extension allows the pass to be made in the fewest steps, and, along with every other phase of the exchange, must be practiced to perfect the necessary timing.

Relay exchanges are divided into two different types: *the visual pass* and *the non-visual, or blind, pass.* In the relays where the incoming runner may experience the greatest fatigue, such as the 4 × 400s, the 4 × 800s and the 4 × 1,500s,

The key to a successful relay is proper baton passing.

the outgoing runner must watch him for a change of speed, and the visual pass should be used. During the sprint relay, the 4 × 100, when the incoming runner ideally comes in at full speed, the outgoing runner takes a blind pass, not looking back as he receives the baton, so that he can leave at full speed, too.

THE VISUAL PASS

In the visual pass, the outgoing runner, or receiver, must first gauge the speed of the incoming runner and then look ahead to see where he is going. He should next turn his head, upper body, and arm back toward the incoming runner to receive the baton. *It is up to the receiver to snatch the baton from the passer's hand.* He can do this by using a palm-down position, a palm-up position, or

The Visual Pass

D

C

H

G

a palm facing to the side position. The receiver's eyes should be on the hand of the passer and he should clutch the baton as soon as he can. Again, *the important point to remember is that the receiver must run at the same speed as the passer.* The receiver should be standing at the near end of the receiving zone, which is 20 meters long, and start his take-off when the incoming runner is five meters away.

The visual pass begins with the receiver in the near end of the receiving zone, gauging the speed of the incoming runner (A). When the incoming runner is 5 meters away, the receiver turns and starts his takeoff (B,C). The receiver then turns his head, arm, and upper body back to receive the baton (D). The receiver watches the baton and extends his arm (E). The incoming runner watches the receiver's palm and extends his arm toward it (F). The receiver grasps the baton (G) and transfers it to his other hand (H). The pass is completed!

B

A

F

E

THE BLIND PASS

In teaching the blind pass, we like to use the overhand pass, in which the passer lays the baton down in the receiver's palm. This way the receiver does not have to change hands, but still has the long end of the baton facing out to pass to the next man. With this method, the first man carries the baton in his right hand and runs close to the line on the curve. The second man carries the baton in his left hand while running the straightaway. The third man carries the baton in his right hand running close to the line on the curve. The anchorman carries the baton in his left hand on the final straightaway. Each exchange should be made in the middle of the lane so that neither athlete will be on the line or out of his lane and risk disqualification. With this type of pass, the receiver does not switch the baton from one hand to another, so the chances of losing time or dropping it are minimized.

Some teams have been successful using a pass in which the baton is placed in the receiver's hand using an upward motion with the receiver's palm facing down, but still, for the long end of the stick to face the next receiver, the runner must switch hands.

In the 4 × 200 meter relay, many teams use the blind pass, but we suggest a fast visual pass. We consider this less risky since many 200-meter runners fade at the end of the run. If the receiver goes out hard when the passer hits a certain mark, he may run away from the passer and either go out of the zone or have to slow down and wait for the incoming runner.

We do not recommend the use of voice signals on sprint passes to tell the receiver to put his hand back. Many times all runners are yelling signals in a race, which creates mass confusion. It is up to the receiver to be at full speed within the receiving zone and then put his hand back.

THE ZONE

When using the blind pass, the team should take advantage of the international or acceleration zone, which is 10 meters long. When the incoming runner is 7 to 8 meters from the restraining line or the acceleration zone end line, the outgoing runner should take off at full speed. He should pump his left arm four times and then put it back with the palm up to receive the pass. By this time, he should have run 15 meters, reaching the same speed as the incoming runner. The exchange should be made about 18 meters into the zone. Once the outgoing runner puts his hand back, he should keep it steady until he feels the baton in his hand. He then closes his hand and continues to run at the same speed. The incoming runner should continue running down the track and not veer out of his lane. If the outgoing runner is receiving the baton in his left hand, he should stay to the right of the lane and the incoming runner should stay to the left so that their legs will not tangle and their arms will not hit each other. The 1984 Southern Illinois 4 × 400 relay team lost the NCAA race because of a right-to-right pass. Elvis Forde stepped on Michael Franks's foot and Franks fell down. He bounced up but was still 10 meters back, and placed second instead of being NCAA champion. That might happen only once in 1,000 times, but it's the one you always remember.

In the middle of the passing zone, at 20 meters, the receiver should have a marker to sight on. If he does not have the baton by that time, he should ease up, as something might have happened: either he started too soon or the incoming runner is fading. By easing up, he can give the incoming runner a chance to catch him and make the exchange. The exchange *must* be made within the zone, or the runners are disqualified. The 7- or 8-meter target for takeoff may vary from one individual to another and may also vary with practice. All members of the team must decide on which target to use so that each passer or receiver is running at the same speed at the time the pass is made.

The receiver should measure his target by stepping it off wearing the track shoe he competes in to count steps. That way he is always consistent in his steps. He should then put a wide piece of tape down so that he can see the marker from his starting position. He should use a standing start with both feet facing the direction in which he is going, and should not pivot. He should leave at top speed each time to retain consistency.

At the Martin Luther King Games in 1976, Auburn had an excellent 4 × 100 meter relay team that ran under 40 seconds every time out, and we all felt they could run faster if everything went well. It didn't. Before the race, I told the team to be sure to measure their targets correctly, place a mark in the zone at 20 meters where they should slow up if they didn't have the baton, run as well as possible . . . and we would win. Our lead-off man, Tony Easley, ran well around the curve. John Lewter took off well, received a good baton pass, and then ran toward Willie Smith. For some reason, however, Willie didn't move until John was right on him. Luckily, Willie didn't put his hand out until John was in the zone, but John was slowing up considerably so he wouldn't run past Willie. Willie did get the baton, and his pass to Harvey Glance was good. Harvey moved us from fifth place to second. Our time was 39.6, and I was disappointed, so I felt I should at least find out what happened to Willie. Did

The Blind Pass

The receiver, at the back of the acceleration zone, starts the pass sequence by sighting the incoming runner when the latter is 20 or so meters away (A). When the incoming runner is 7 to 8 meters away, the receiver begins his sprint (B,C).

A

B

C

D

After pumping his left arm four times, the receiver puts it back to receive the baton, palm upward (D). The incoming runner slaps the baton smoothly into the receiver's outstretched hand (E), and the receiver, at full speed by now, is off and running (F). The blind pass is most effective in the 4 × 100 relay, but it requires a great deal of practice to work properly.

E

F

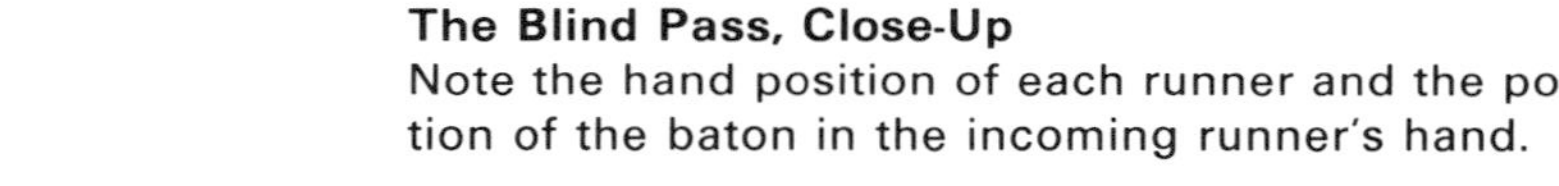

The Blind Pass, Close-Up
Note the hand position of each runner and the position of the baton in the incoming runner's hand.

he slip? Was his marker in the wrong spot? What happened? Willie said, "I watched the marker, but John stepped over it so I didn't get started." I said, "Did you expect him to go back and touch it?" Sometimes the reality of a situation—not your plan—must dictate your response in a relay.

RELAY ORDER

Choosing the order of runners in the longer relays depends on many factors. Usually, a team's best and most competitive man runs anchor, and the next best man leads off to get the team out in good position. The weakest man normally runs second, so that if he gets behind, the third man can make up ground. The order may be changed depending on the strength of the opposition in the longer relays because visual passes can be practiced in different order throughout the practice sessions. But in the sprint relay a team should set an order and stick with it. Passers and receivers must learn to know each other. They learn how fast each passer comes in, how hard he places the baton in the receiver's hand, and the position of the outgoing hand (is it held high or low?). Sometimes a team may change its order if it is not reaching its potential or is habitually making mistakes. For a sprint relay, the usual order, again, is best man as the anchor, and the next-best, who must also be a good starter, first. When placing the other two runners, a good baton handler and curve runner should run the third leg and a good baton handler and straightaway runner should go second.

The U.S. team at the 1983 World Championships in Helsinki demonstrates good relay order. Carl Lewis, considered the world's fastest at the time, anchored the team to victory. Calvin Smith, perhaps the second-fastest then, was strategically placed third, running the final curve as he does so well (witness his 200-meter world championship). Emmitt King, third in the 100 meters, is considered by many to have the fastest start in the world and was the natural choice for the lead-off position. Not to be left out, Willie Gault, a great straightaway runner from his hurdling experience, ran the second leg on the straight. The world record they set, 37.86, wasn't beaten until the 1984 Olympic Games.

Some people wondered, however, if the fastest quartet ever assembled would get its act together in Los Angeles. Lewis, the Olympic champion, was anchoring, runner-up Sam Graddy was leading off, Ron Brown, the fourth-place finisher in the 1984 Olympics 100 meters, was running second, and Smith, the world record holder in the 100 meters, was running the third leg around the curve. As they approached the first round, they were tight as drums. I said, "Relax, fellas, you're running against Qatar," but that didn't loosen them up.

Their baton handoffs were horrible since they didn't want to run out of the zone and were trying to play it extra safe. Nevertheless, they ran 38.85 and won easily. In the semifinal, they were a little better and ran 38.42. I finally got them together and explained that they had to have faith in their marks. "Use the safety zone if necessary," I said, "and you should win the race easily." They had a good pass on the first exchange and the last two passes were excellent. With their speed, they broke the world record with a time of 37.83. The point is, even the best in the world get tight when they are being overcautious.

INDOOR RELAYS

Since indoor tracks are often narrow and hard to pass on, many teams lead off with their best man to establish position and to let his teammates run free and out of traffic. Again, this would be a strategy decision based on the type of runners composing a relay and whether they run better from the front or coming from behind. Though he may be the fastest runner, the lead-off man must also be an excellent starter, for he usually runs in lanes anywhere from 50 meters to 150 meters depending on the size of the track. Before the second man can break to the inside, he must be able to run in a crowd, and the third man must be able to run well in front. As always, the anchor man should be a strong competitor.

RELAY PRACTICE

We recommend practice for the visual relays at least once a week. We break off into groups of four to six and run up and down the straightaway working on half-speed handoffs. We change the order of the group in each session, just as we might in a meet with the longer relays.

In selecting our personnel for the sprint relay, we run a 100-meter time trial to rank our fastest people. The first four will be our team and the next two will be the alternates. We consider this the fairest method, one that fosters team morale.

We schedule our practices for the sprint relay at the start of practice each day before the runners branch off into their specific areas, especially if we have a sprinter, a hurdler, a long jumper, and a 400-meter man combining on the team. We choose to work on relays at the beginning of practice so that fatigue will not be a factor as we practice our handoffs.

We recommend that teams start by placing four to six men single-file in a stationary line and have them hand off by pumping their arms four times and then putting their hand back. The baton is then passed back to the first man. After about ten minutes of this drill, the runners should spread themselves about 25 meters apart and hand off running at half-speed. After four passes in this manner, the runners go to the zone on the straightaway and work on the following exchanges three times each at three quarters speed: first man to second man, third man to fourth man, second man to third man. Alternates and substitutes should also practice these routines so that they will have some practice experience if they are needed.

Another drill we do at Auburn is to have the runners jog around the track

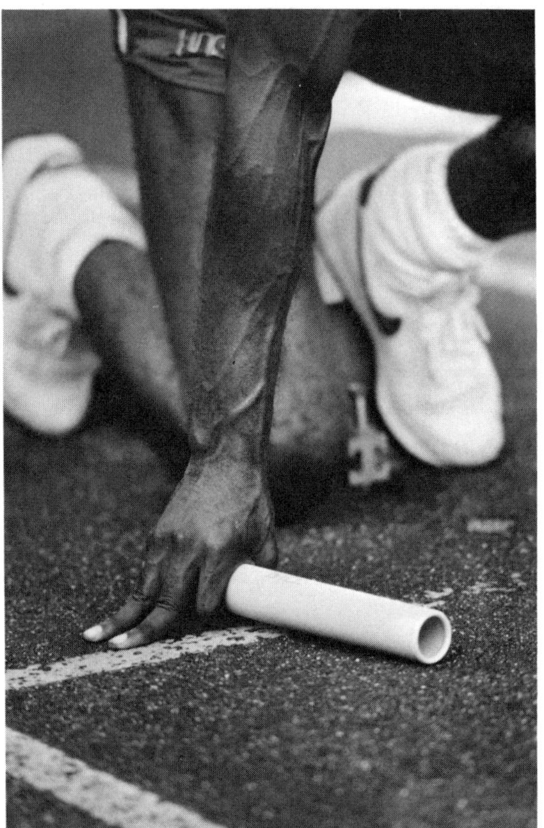

Holding the Baton at the Start
Most lead-off runners hold the end of the baton with their thumb and forefinger, and position the middle finger behind the starting line (as shown here). Their grip is very tight lest they throw or drop the baton at the gun.

taking handoffs until they have completed two laps. When the anchorman gets the baton, he hands it back up the line instead of dropping it on the ground for the lead-off man to pick up. This eliminates the chance of the lead-off man straining by having to reach down for the baton.

Still another drill is a five-man relay where each runner runs 100 meters and hands off. He strides until he is 20 meters from the zone and then runs hard during the pass. Each runner should run four times.

STARTING THE RELAY

The lead-off runner in any relay where each man runs a leg of 800 meters or more should hold the baton firmly in his hand across his chest while in a standing position so that it can't get knocked out of his hand at the start.

The lead-off man running 400 meters or less should use a crouch start and should hold the baton in his hand with one or two fingers, whichever feels more comfortable to him. He should hold it very tight so that he doesn't throw it or drop it as he sprints out of the blocks.

Success

Your number one goal in running is, of course, to run faster than the opposition. If you can win, then your next goal is to run record times. Our goal for the athlete is simply to win, because as long as he is winning, the performances will come. We always say, "Win every race and you will be the Olympic champion"—and it's true, because as you win you go on to tougher competition. The usual progression is: time trial, dual meets, relay meets, conference meets, national meets, Olympic Trials, and finally, the Olympic Games.

Your goal should always be to be the best you can. If you compete at your best and run your best performance, then that's all that can be expected. If you do your best, you boost your self-esteem. When your best on a given day is also the best you've ever done, that's called a personal record, or PR. Winning is important, but if you can get a PR in a loss, then you still will have been successful. *You can be a winner even if you aren't the first across the finish line.*

Success comes from making effort all the way. A champion is born a champion, but to succeed he still has to do all his workouts. Some athletes have all the tools but throw them away by not getting themselves ready.

For any Olympic runner a gold medal is a tangible reward for hard work and dedication.

Over the years we've developed ten cardinal principles of training and competition, some of which we touched upon earlier, but all of which we'd like to summarize here. Adhering to these ten should bring success.

1. *Never run at full speed in practice, except during starts and wind sprints.* Instead, work at 75 to 90 percent effort, concentrating on good running mechanics. Running all-out can produce injury, and the key to your success is staying healthy. A slightly undertrained, healthy athlete will beat an overtrained, injured athlete every time out.

2. *Limit your number of races and make them all good ones.* Since a meet is your chance to put in your best racing effort, point your training toward the meets and ease off on hard training as the meet approaches. At the same time, concentrate on your key events during a meet and don't overrace. How many times have we seen a top athlete pull up during his fourth or fifth race in a meet? To repeat: Limit your number of races and make them all good ones. There's another reason, besides injury, for trying not to do too much in a meet. Harrison "Bones" Dillard, the 1948 Olympic 100-meter champion, overextended himself in an AAU meet in Milwaukee and ruined his streak of eighty-two consecutive victories in the 110-meter hurdles. He tried to run four races within 67 minutes, and first lost the 100 meters and then lost the 110-meter hurdles.

3. *Whether in practice or in a meet, always warm up and warm down.* The warmup gets you ready while the warmdown ends the workout or race on a positive note and keeps the muscles from being stiff the next day.

4. *Do only steady, static stretching.* Along with the warmup and warmdown, this stretching is a necessity and should be done before and after each race. It's not unusual for an athlete to go through two or three warmup and warmdown sessions at a meet.

5. *Always run a qualifying race as well as you can.* Try to run each race both hard and relaxed to keep your intensity consistent. We think it is important to qualify well, both for the psychological effect and perhaps for a better lane in the next race, if the lanes are assigned according to performance. In other words, a 10.1 sprinter should not run 10.7 in the 100-meter trials. He should run a relaxed 10.3.

6. *Always maintain good form when running.* Maintaining good form throughout a race often will lead to victory. Races are won not by increasing speed at the end, but rather by not slowing down. Concentrate on not straining

or tying up and on holding form through the finish, and always lean at the end of a sprint.

7. *Study your week and race plan, and plan your workouts accordingly in preparation for your next meet.* After you finish a race on the weekend, go light for at least one day to clear the lactic acid buildup out of the legs. Work harder earlier in the training cycle (which can be one to two weeks long, depending on when your next meet is scheduled) and ease off as the meet approaches.

8. *Work on your sprint skills each week, making sure you work on form, drills, starts, baton-passing, and other skills pertaining to running fast in your event.*

9. *Do weight training, even during the competitive season.* The strength you build earlier in the year can be maintained by training at least twice a week, with fewer repetitions at a heavier weight.

10. *Keep your practice sessions fun.* Encourage friendly competition at all times, especially as you and your teammates come out of the blocks or practice your leans at the finish line during workout drills.

COMMUNICATION

One means to success is communication between coach and athlete. We're always fascinated by the middle-distance coach who can show the workouts his athletes will be doing two years from now to the day. *This loss of respect for individual needs is a sure sign of a communications breakdown between athlete and coach.* We used to laugh at the stories told about the late Villanova coach, Jumbo Elliot, when people tried to understand his system. "Some days we did more 440s and some days we did fewer," one runner summed up. Jumbo's approach was so simple, yet revealed so much about the man. Elliot was a master coach because he sensed what his athletes needed and when, so they would be ready. If you're a coach, never forget: your athletes are human. Put yourself in their shoes and always try to understand their needs. The best coaches in the world are human, too.

Athletes and coaches alike are human, and communication between them is critical to each's success.

A SPORT FOR ALL SEASONS

In the United States, the track athlete has to be ready for two major seasons —indoors and outdoors—and three if you count cross-country. In many parts of the country, indoor track is downplayed because the good weather allows for a longer outdoor season. In the Northeast, however, indoor track is a matter of survival as well as a means to outstanding competition.

Indoor track is worth getting excited about. For the middle-distance and the distance runner, it presents a wide variety of opportunities, ranging from the 600 to the 1,500 and the 5,000, plus several relays. The season allows needed breaks from training boredom and gives runners a chance to check their speed and progress.

Sometimes track people get obsessed with training and forget that racing and the experience of racing are what the sport is all about. For the lucky few athletes who are invited to Europe or Asia to compete in major summer meets, careful planning will enable them to race from January to September—and enjoy every minute of it. In September 1980, at the end of a long but happy season that had begun nine months earlier, I took a team to Japan and China,

Great runners, such as Evelyn Ashford, are dedicated and, ultimately, self-motivated.

and the 4 × 100 relay team of Harvey Glance, Willie Smith, Stanley Floyd, and Fred Taylor ran the fastest time of the year in beating the Olympic champions from the Soviet Union. These same runners were still outstanding when the next indoor season began in January.

We've offered some ideas and some thoughts on how to run better, but the great track athletes will always be the dedicated self-motivated ones. They're the runners who follow the right training methods and do all the workouts and weight training. They'll always rise to the top. The winners in track are those who have made sacrifices. There are no shortcuts to success.

Appendix: Workouts

The following workouts show two sample weeks of midseason training for each of track's major events. The workouts are the same for any athlete in the given event; the only change is the pace of the runners. If you find the paces not to your liking—either too slow or too fast for your ability—by all means change them, particularly if they are too fast. In general, you should never start any running program without first having a complete medical checkup from a qualified physician, and you then should start gradually and slowly build up your speed, distance, strength, etc., over many months' time.

100 AND 200 METERS
WORKOUT WEEK #1

College and club athletes

Monday 300–200–100–100–200–300 at 14-second pace. Weights.

Tuesday Handoffs. 6 starts running 30 meters. 6 × 100 meters from blocks in 12.5 seconds. Walk between.

Wednesday Handoffs. 4 starts running 30 meters. 3 laps of wind sprints. Weights.

Thursday 3 easy 110s.

Friday Rest.

Saturday Meet.

High school athletes

Monday 300–200–100–100–200–300 at 15-second pace. Weights.

Tuesday Handoffs. 6 starts running 30 meters. 6 × 100 meters from blocks in 13.5 seconds. Walk between.

Wednesday Handoffs. 4 starts running 30 meters. 3 laps of wind sprints. Weights.

Thursday 3 easy 110s.

Friday Rest.

Saturday Meet.

Age–group athletes

Monday 300–200–100–100–200–300 at 17-second pace. Weights.

Tuesday Handoffs. 6 starts running 30 meters. 6 × 100 meters from blocks in 15 seconds. Walk between.

Wednesday Handoffs. 4 starts running 30 meters. 3 laps of wind sprints. Weights.

Thursday 3 easy 110s.

Friday Rest.

Saturday Meet.

Women

Monday 300–200–100–100–200–300 at 18-second pace. Weights.

Tuesday Handoffs. 6 starts running 30 meters. 6 × 100 meters from blocks in 16 seconds. Walk between.

Wednesday Handoffs. 4 starts running 30 meters. 3 laps of wind sprints. Weights.

Thursday 3 easy 110s.

Friday Rest.

Saturday Meet.

WORKOUT WEEK #2

College and club athletes

Monday Handoffs. 3 × 300 in 42 seconds with 300-meter walk between. Weights.
Tuesday Handoffs. 6 starts running 30 meters. 6 × 150 in 20 seconds. Walk between.
Wednesday Handoffs. 6 starts running 30 meters. 6 × 110 in 14 seconds. Walk between. Weights.
Thursday 4 easy 110s.
Friday Rest.
Saturday Meet.

High school athletes

Monday Handoffs. 3 × 300 in 45 seconds with 300-meter walk. Weights.
Tuesday Handoffs. 6 starts running 30 meters. 6 × 150 in 22 seconds. Walk between.
Wednesday Handoffs. 6 starts running 30 meters. 6 × 110 in 16 seconds. Walk between. Weights.
Thursday 4 easy 110s.
Friday Rest.
Saturday Meet.

Age–group athletes

Monday Handoffs. 3 × 300 in 51 seconds with 300-meter walk between. Weights.
Tuesday Handoffs. 6 starts running 30 meters. 6 × 150 in 25 seconds. Walk between.
Wednesday Handoffs. 6 starts running 30 meters. 6 × 110 in 18 seconds. Walk between. Weights.
Thursday 4 easy 110s.
Friday Rest.
Saturday Meet.

Women

Monday Handoffs. 3 × 300 in 54 seconds with 300-meter walk between. Weights.
Tuesday Handoffs. 6 starts running 30 meters. 6 × 150 in 27 seconds. Walk between.
Wednesday Handoffs. 6 starts running 30 meters. 6 × 110 in 20 seconds. Walk between. Weights.
Thursday 4 easy 110s.
Friday Rest.
Saturday Meet.

400 METERS

WORKOUT WEEK #1

College and club athletes

Monday 500–400–300 run at 14-second pace. Walk between. Weights.
Tuesday 4 starts running 30 meters. 200–100–100–200 at 12.5-second pace. Walk between.
Wednesday 4 starts running 30 meters. 4 laps of wind sprints. Weights.
Thursday 1,600-meter relay handoffs. 4 easy 110s.
Friday Rest.
Saturday Meet.

High school athletes

Monday 500–400–300 run at 15-second pace. Walk between. Weights.
Tuesday 4 starts running 30 meters. 200–100–100–200 at 13.5-second pace. Walk between.
Wednesday 4 starts running 30 meters. 4 laps of wind sprints. Weights.
Thursday 1,600-meter relay handoffs. 4 easy 110s.
Friday Rest.
Saturday Meet.

Age–group athletes

Monday 500–400–300 ran at 17-second pace. Walk between. Weights.
Tuesday 4 starts running 30 meters. 200–100–100–200 at 16-second pace. Walk between.
Wednesday 4 starts running 30 meters. 4 laps of wind sprints. Weights.
Thursday 1,600-meter relay handoffs. 4 easy 110s.
Friday Rest.
Saturday Meet.

Women

Monday 500–400–300 run at 18-second pace. Walk between. Weights.
Tuesday 4 starts running 30 meters. 200–100–100–200 at 17-second pace. Walk between.
Wednesday 4 starts running 30 meters. 4 laps of wind sprints. Weights.
Thursday 1,600-meter relay handoffs. 4 easy 110s.
Friday Rest.
Saturday Meet.

400 METERS
WORKOUT WEEK #2

College and club athletes

Monday 4 × 300 in 42 seconds with 300-meter walk between. Weights.

Tuesday 4 starts running 30 meters. 3 × 200 in 24 seconds. Walk between.

Wednesday 4 starts running 30 meters. 6 × 110 in 14 seconds. Walk between. Weights.

Thursday 1,600-meter relay handoffs. 4 easy 110s.

Friday Rest.

Saturday Meet.

High school athletes

Monday 4 × 300 in 45 seconds with 300-meter walk between. Weights.

Tuesday 4 starts running 30 meters. 3 × 200 in 26 seconds. Walk between.

Wednesday 4 starts running 30 meters. 6 × 110 in 16 seconds. Walk between. Weights.

Thursday 1,600-meter relay handoffs. 4 easy 110s.

Friday Rest.

Saturday Meet.

Age–group athletes

Monday 4 × 300 in 51 seconds with 300-meter walk between. Weights.

Tuesday 4 starts running 30 meters. 3 × 200 in 30 seconds. Walk between.

Wednesday 4 starts running 30 meters. 6 × 110 in 18 seconds. Walk between. Weights.

Thursday 1,600-meter relay handoffs. 4 easy 110s.

Friday Rest.

Saturday Meet.

Women

Monday 4 × 300 in 54 seconds with 300-meter walk between. Weights.

Tuesday 4 starts running 30 meters. 3 × 200 in 32 seconds. Walk between.

Wednesday 4 starts running 30 meters. 6 × 110 in 19 seconds. Walk between. Weights.

Thursday 1,600-meter relay handoffs. 4 easy 110s.

Friday Rest.

Saturday Meet.

110-METER HIGH HURDLES
WORKOUT WEEK #1

College and club athletes

Monday 6 hurdles 9 yards apart. 6 × 300–200–100–100–200–300 at 15-second pace. Walk between. Weights.

Tuesday 4 starts running 30 meters. 4 × 4 high hurdles, regular distance. 4 × 100 in 12.5 seconds. Walk between.

Wednesday 4 laps of wind sprints. Weights.

Thursday 4 easy 110s.

Friday Rest.

Saturday Meet.

High school athletes

Monday 6 hurdles 9 yards apart. 6 × 300–200–100–100–200–300 at 16-second pace. Walk between. Weights.

Tuesday 4 starts running 30 meters. 4 × 4 HH, regular distance. 4 × 100 in 13.5 seconds. Walk between.

Wednesday 4 laps of wind sprints. Weights.

Thursday 4 easy 110s.

Friday Rest.

Saturday Meet.

Age-group athletes

Monday 6 hurdles 9 yards apart. 6 × 300–200–100–100–200–300 at 17-second pace. Walk between. Weights.

Tuesday 4 starts running 30 meters. 4 × 4 HH, regular distance. 4 × 100 in 15 seconds. Walk between.

Wednesday 4 laps of wind sprints. Weights.

Thursday 4 easy 110s.

Friday Rest.

Saturday Meet.

Women

Monday 6 hurdles 9 yards apart. 6 × 300–200–100–100–200–300 at 18-second pace. Walk between. Weights.

Tuesday 4 starts running 30 meters. 4 × 4 HH, regular distance. 4 × 100 in 16 seconds. Walk between.

Wednesday 4 laps of wind sprints. Weights.

Thursday 4 easy 110s.

Friday Rest.

Saturday Meet.

110-METER HIGH HURDLES
WORKOUT WEEK #2

College and club athletes

Monday 12 hurdles 9 yards apart 4 times. 2 × 300 in 42 seconds. Walk between. Weights.

Tuesday 4 starts running 30 meters. 5 hurdles, regular distance 4 times. 4 × 150 in 20 seconds. Walk between.

Wednesday 4 starts running 30 meters. 3 hurdles, regular distance 4 times. 6 × 110 in 14 seconds. Walk between. Weights.

Thursday 4 easy 110s.

Friday Rest.

Saturday Meet.

High school athletes

Monday 12 hurdles 9 yards apart 4 times. 2 × 300 in 45 seconds. Walk between. Weights.

Tuesday 4 starts running 30 meters. 5 hurdles, regular distance 4 times. 4 × 150 in 22 seconds. Walk between.

Wednesday 4 starts running 30 meters. 3 hurdles, regular distance 4 times. 6 × 110 in 14 seconds. Walk between. Weights.

Thursday 4 easy 110s.

Friday Rest.

Saturday Meet.

Age–group athletes

Monday 12 hurdles 9 yards apart 4 times. 2 × 300 in 48 seconds. Walk between. Weights.

Tuesday 4 starts running 30 meters. 5 hurdles, regular distance 4 times. 4 × 150 in 24 seconds. Walk between.

Wednesday 4 starts running 30 meters. 3 hurdles, regular distance 4 times. 6 × 110 in 16 seconds. Walk between. Weights.

Thursday 4 easy 110s.

Friday Rest.

Saturday Meet.

Women

Monday 12 hurdles 9 yards apart 4 times. 2 × 300 in 51 seconds. Walk between. Weights.

Tuesday 4 starts running 30 meters. 5 hurdles, regular distance 4 times. 4 × 150 in 26 seconds. Walk between.

Wednesday 4 starts running 30 meters. 3 hurdles, regular distance 4 times. 6 × 110 in 17 seconds. Walk between. Weights.

Thursday 4 easy 110s.

Friday Rest.

Saturday Meet.

400-METER INTERMEDIATE HURDLES

WORKOUT WEEK #1

College and club athletes

Monday 4 × 4 IH. 500–400–300 run at 14-second pace. Walk between. Weights.

Tuesday 4 × 4 IH. 4 times 1st 3 hurdles. 200–100–100–200 at 12.5-second pace. Walk between.

Wednesday 4 laps of wind sprints. Weights.

Thursday 4 easy 110s.

Friday Rest.

Saturday Meet.

High school athletes

Monday 4 × 4 IH. 500–400–300 run at 15-second pace. Walk between. Weights.

Tuesday 4 × 4 IH. 4 times 1st 3 hurdles. 200–100–100–200 at 13.5-second pace. Walk between.

Wednesday 4 laps of wind sprints. Weights.

Thursday 4 easy 110s.

Friday Rest.

Saturday Meet.

Age–group athletes

Monday 4 × 4 IH. 500–400–300 run at 17-second pace. Walk between. Weights.

Tuesday 4 × 4 IH. 4 times 1st 3 hurdles. 200–100–100–200 at 16-second pace. Walk between.

Wednesday 4 laps of wind sprints. Weights.

Thursday 4 easy 110s.

Friday Rest.

Saturday Meet.

Women

Monday 4 × 4 IH. 500–400–300 run at 18-second pace. Walk between. Weights.

Tuesday 4 × 4 IH. 4 times 1st 3 hurdles. 200–100–100–200 at 17-second pace. Walk between.

Wednesday 4 laps of wind sprints. Weights.

Thursday 4 easy 110s.

Friday Rest.

Saturday Meet.

400-METER INTERMEDIATE HURDLES
WORKOUT WEEK #2

College and club athletes

Monday 4 × 4 IH. 4 × 300 in 42 seconds with 300-meter walk between. Weights.

Tuesday 4 starts running 30 meters. 2 × 7 IH going thru 1st 200 in 25 seconds. 15 minutes rest between.

Wednesday 4 starts running 30 meters. 4 times 1st 4 IH. 3 × 110 in 14 seconds. Walk between. Weights.

Thursday 4 easy 110s.

Friday Rest.

Saturday Meet.

High school athletes

Monday 4 × 4 IH. 4 × 300 in 45 seconds with 300-meter walk between. Weights.

Tuesday 4 starts running 30 meters. 2 × 7 IH going thru 1st 200 in 27 seconds. 15 minute rest between.

Wednesday 4 starts running 30 meters. 4 times 1st 4 IH. 3 × 110 in 16 seconds. Walk between. Weights.

Thursday 4 easy 110s.

Friday Rest.

Saturday Meet.

Age–group athletes

Monday 4 × 4 IH. 4 × 300 in 51 seconds with 300-meter walk between. Weights.

Tuesday 4 starts running 30 meters. 2 × 7 IH going thru 1st 200 in 32 seconds. 15 minutes rest between.

Wednesday 4 starts running 30 meters. 4 times 1st 4 IH. 3 × 110 in 18 seconds. Walk between. Weights.

Thursday 4 easy 110s.

Friday Rest.

Saturday Meet.

Women

Monday 4 × 4 IH. 4 × 300 in 54 seconds with 300-meter walk between. Weights.

Tuesday 4 starts running 30 meters. 2 × 7 IH going thru 1st 200 in 34 seconds. 15 minute rest between.

Wednesday 4 starts running 30 meters. 4 times 1st 4 IH. 3 × 110 in 19 seconds. Walk between. Weights.

Thursday 4 easy 110s.

Friday Rest.

Saturday Meet.

800 METERS
WORKOUT WEEK #1

College and club athletes

Monday 2 × 600 in 1:30. 4 minute recovery. 4 × 300 in 45 seconds. 300-meter jog between. Weights.

Tuesday Easy distance day, 6 miles. 6 × 100 pickups. No time.

Wednesday 3 × 400 in 58 seconds. 5 minute rest between. 3 × 300 in 42 seconds. 5 minute rest between. 3 × 200 in 28 seconds. Walk between. Weights.

Thursday Easy distance day, 6 miles.

Friday Easy distance day, 4 miles.

Saturday Meet.

Sunday Easy distance day, 6 miles.

High school athletes

Monday 2 × 600 in 1:36. 4 minute recovery. 4 × 300 in 48 seconds. 300-meter jog between. Weights.

Tuesday Easy distance day, 6 miles. 6 × 100 pickups. No time.

Wednesday 3 × 400 in 62 seconds. 5 minute rest between. 3 × 300 in 45 seconds. 5 minute rest between. 3 × 200 in 30 seconds. Walk between. Weights.

Thursday Easy distance day, 6 miles.

Friday Easy distance day, 4 miles.

Saturday Meet.

Sunday Easy distance day, 6 miles.

Age–group athletes

Monday 2 × 600 in 1:42. 4 minute recovery. 4 × 300 in 51 seconds. 300-meter jog between. Weights.

Tuesday Easy distance day, 6 miles. 6 × 100 pickups. No time.

Wednesday 3 × 400 in 66 seconds. 5 minute rest between. 3 × 300 in 48 seconds. 5 minute rest between. 3 × 200 in 32 seconds. Walk between. Weights.

Thursday Easy distance day, 6 miles.

Friday Easy distance day, 4 miles.

Saturday Meet.

Sunday Easy distance day, 6 miles.

Women

Monday 2 × 600 in 1:48. 4 minute recovery. 4 × 300 in 54 seconds. 300-meter jog between. Weights.

Tuesday Easy distance day, 6 miles. 6 × 100 pickups. No time.

Wednesday 3 × 400 in 70 seconds. 5 minute rest between. 3 × 300 in 51 seconds. 5 minute rest between. 3 × 200 in 34 seconds. Walk between. Weights.

Thursday Easy distance day, 6 miles.

Friday Easy distance day, 4 miles.

Saturday Meet.

Sunday Easy distance day, 6 miles.

College and club athletes

Monday 3 × 400 in 56 seconds. 4 minute recovery. 6 × 300 in 42 seconds. 300-meter jog between. Weights.

Tuesday 6 mile run. 6 × 150 in 20 seconds. Jog between.

Wednesday 4 × 300 in 42 seconds. 5 minute rest between. 4 × 200 in 26 seconds. Jog between. Weights.

Thursday Easy 4 miles. 4 × 100 strides.

Friday Easy 3 miles.

Saturday Meet.

Sunday Easy distance day, 6 miles.

High school athletes

Monday 3 × 400 in 60 seconds. 4 minute recovery. 6 × 300 in 45 seconds. 300-meter jog between. Weights.

Tuesday 6 mile run. 6 × 150 in 22 seconds. Jog between.

Wednesday 4 × 300 in 45 seconds. 5 minute rest between. 4 × 200 in 28 seconds. 200-meter jog between. Weights.

Thursday Easy 4 miles. 4 × 100 strides.

Friday Easy 3 miles.

Saturday Meet.

Sunday Easy distance day, 6 miles.

Age–group athletes

Monday 3 × 400 in 66 seconds. 4 minute recovery. 6 × 300 in 48 seconds. 300-meter jog between. Weights.

Tuesday 6 mile run. 6 × 150 in 24 seconds. Jog between.

Wednesday 4 × 300 in 48 seconds. 5 minute rest. 4 × 200 in 30 seconds. 200-meter jog between. Weights.

Thursday Easy 4 miles. 4 × 100 strides.

Friday Easy 3 miles.

Saturday Meet.

Sunday Easy distance day, 6 miles.

Women

Monday 3 × 400 in 70 seconds. 4 minute recovery. 6 × 300 in 51 seconds. 300-meter jog between. Weights.

Tuesday 6 mile run. 6 × 150 in 26 seconds. Jog between.

Wednesday 4 × 300 in 51 seconds. 5 minute rest. 4 × 200 in 32 seconds. 200-meter jog between. Weights.

Thursday Easy 4 miles. 4 × 100 strides.

Friday Easy 3 miles.

Saturday Meet.

Sunday Easy distance day, 6 miles.

1,500 METERS
WORKOUT WEEK #1

College and club athletes

Monday 4 × 600 in 1:36. 600-meter jog between. 4 × 300 in 45 seconds. 300-meter jog between.

Tuesday Easy distance day, 7 miles. Weights.

Wednesday 6 × 1,200 in 3:30. 3 minute jog between.

Thursday Easy 6 miles.

Friday Easy 4 miles.

Saturday Meet.

Sunday Easy distance day, 10 miles. Weights.

High school athletes

Monday 4 × 600 in 1:42. 600-meter jog between. 4 × 300 in 48 seconds. 300-meter jog between.

Tuesday Easy distance day, 7 miles. Weights.

Wednesday 6 × 1,200 in 3:45. 3 minute jog between.

Thursday Easy 6 miles.

Friday Easy 4 miles.

Saturday Meet.

Sunday Easy distance day, 10 miles. Weights.

Age–group athletes

Monday 4 × 600 in 1:48. 600-meter jog between. 4 × 300 in 51 seconds. 300-meter jog between.

Tuesday Easy distance day, 7 miles. Weights.

Wednesday 6 × 1,200 in 4:00. 3 minute jog between.

Thursday Easy 6 miles.

Friday Easy 4 miles.

Saturday Meet.

Sunday Easy distance day, 10 miles. Weights.

Women

Monday 4 × 600 in 1:54. 600-meter jog between. 4 × 300 in 54 seconds. 300-meter jog between.

Tuesday Easy distance day, 7 miles. Weights.

Wednesday 6 × 1,200 in 4:20. 3 minute jog between.

Thursday Easy 6 miles.

Friday Easy 4 miles.

Saturday Meet.

Sunday Easy distance day, 10 miles. Weights.

ALL RUNNERS: Monday-Tuesday-Wednesday-Thursday at 6 to 7 A.M. take an easy 4-mile run at 7-minute to 8-minute pace.

1,500 METERS
WORKOUT WEEK #2

College and club athletes

Monday 4 × 800 in 2:06. 800-meter jog between. Rest 10 minutes. 4 × 400 in 62 seconds. 400-meter jog between.

Tuesday Easy 8 miles. Weights.

Wednesday 6 × 300 in 45 seconds. 300-meter jog between. Rest 5 minutes. 6 × 200 in 30 seconds. 200-meter jog between.

Thursday Easy 6 miles.

Friday Easy 4 miles.

Saturday Meet.

Sunday Easy 10-mile run. Weights.

High school athletes

Monday 4 × 800 in 2:12. 800-meter jog between. Rest 10 minutes. 4 × 400 in 66 seconds. 400-meter jog between.

Tuesday Easy 8 miles. Weights.

Wednesday 6 × 300 in 48 seconds. 300-meter jog between. Rest 5 minutes. 6 × 200 in 32 seconds. 200-meter jog between.

Thursday Easy 6 miles.

Friday Easy 4 miles.

Saturday Meet.

Sunday Easy 10-mile run. Weights.

Age–group athletes

Monday 4 × 800 in 2:20. 800-meter jog between. Rest 10 minutes. 4 × 400 in 70 seconds. 400-meter jog between.

Tuesday Easy 8 miles. Weights.

Wednesday 6 × 300 in 51 seconds. 300-meter jog between. Rest 5 minutes. 6 × 200 in 34 seconds. 200-meter jog between.

Thursday Easy 6 miles.

Friday Easy 4 miles.

Saturday Meet.

Sunday Easy 10-mile run. Weights.

Women

Monday 4 × 800 in 2:30. 800-meter jog between. Rest 10 minutes. 4 × 400 in 76 seconds. 400-meter jog between.

Tuesday Easy 8 miles. Weights.

Wednesday 6 × 300 in 54 seconds. 300-meter jog. Rest 5 minutes. 6 × 200 in 36 seconds. 200-meter jog between.

Thursday Easy 6 miles.

Friday Easy 4 miles.

Saturday Meet.

Sunday Easy 10-mile run. Weights.

ALL RUNNERS: Monday-Tuesday-Wednesday-Thursday at 6 to 7 A.M. take an easy 4-mile run at 7-minute to 8-minute pace.

5,000 METERS

WORKOUT WEEK #1

College and club athletes

Monday 4 × 800 in 2:16, 800-meter jog between. 2 × 400 in 62 seconds. 400-meter jog between.

Tuesday Easy distance day, 8 miles. Weights.

Wednesday 6 × 1,200 in 3:45. 3 minute recovery between.

Thursday Easy 6 miles.

Friday Easy 4 miles.

Saturday Meet.

Sunday Easy distance day, 12 miles. Weights.

High school athletes

Monday 4 × 800 in 2:24. 800-meter jog between. 2 × 400 in 66 seconds. 400-meter jog between.

Tuesday Easy distance day, 8 miles. Weights.

Wednesday 6 × 1,200 in 4:00. 3 minute recovery between.

Thursday Easy 6 miles.

Friday Easy 4 miles.

Saturday Meet.

Sunday Easy distance day, 12 miles. Weights.

Age–group athletes

Monday 4 × 800 in 2:32. 800-meter jog between. 2 × 400 in 70 seconds. 400-meter jog between.

Tuesday Easy distance day, 8 miles. Weights.

Wednesday 6 × 1,200 in 4:20. 3 minute recovery between.

Thursday Easy 6 miles.

Friday Easy 4 miles.

Saturday Meet.

Sunday Easy distance day, 12 miles. Weights.

Women

Monday 4 × 800 in 2:40. 800-meter jog between. 2 × 400 in 74 seconds. 400-meter jog between.

Tuesday Easy distance day, 8 miles. Weights.

Wednesday 6 × 1,200 in 4:40. 3 minute recovery between.

Thursday Easy 6 miles.

Friday Easy 4 miles.

Saturday Meet.

Sunday Easy distance day, 12 miles. Weights.

ALL RUNNERS: Monday-Tuesday-Wednesday-Thursday at 6 to 7 A.M. take an easy 4-mile run at 7-minute to 8-minute pace.

STEEPLECHASE RUNNERS follow same pattern, but do Monday's interval work over barriers at a pace two seconds slower on each lap.

5,000 METERS
WORKOUT WEEK #2

College and club athletes

Monday 4 × 600 in 1:39. 600-meter jog. Rest 10 minutes. 4 × 300 in 48 seconds. 300-meter jog between.

Tuesday Easy 8 miles. Weights.

Wednesday 6 × 400 in 64 seconds. Rest 5 minutes. 4 × 200 in 30 seconds. 200-meter jog.

Thursday Easy 6 miles.

Friday Easy 4 miles.

Saturday Meet.

Sunday Easy 12 miles. Weights.

High school athletes

Monday 4 × 600 in 1:45. 600-meter jog. Rest 10 minutes. 4 × 300 in 48 seconds. 300-meter jog between.

Tuesday Easy 8 miles. Weights.

Wednesday 6 × 400 in 68 seconds. Rest 5 minutes. 4 × 200 in 32 seconds. 200-meter jog.

Thursday Easy 6 miles.

Friday Easy 4 miles.

Saturday Meet.

Sunday Easy 12 miles. Weights.

Age–group athletes

Monday 4 × 600 in 1:52. 600-meter jog. Rest 10 minutes. 4 × 300 in 51 seconds. 300-meter jog between.

Tuesday Easy 8 miles. Weights.

Wednesday 6 × 400 in 72 seconds. Rest 5 minutes. 4 × 200 in 34 seconds. 200-meter jog between.

Thursday Easy 6 miles.

Friday Easy 4 miles.

Saturday Meet.

Sunday Easy 12 miles. Weights.

Women

Monday 4 × 600 in 2:00. 600-meter jog. Rest 10 minutes. 4 × 300 in 54 seconds. 300-meter jog between.

Tuesday Easy 8 miles. Weights.

Wednesday 6 × 400 in 80 seconds. Rest 5 minutes. 4 × 200 in 36 seconds. 200-meter jog between.

Thursday Easy 6 miles.

Friday Easy 4 miles.

Saturday Meet.

Sunday Easy 12 miles. Weights.

ALL RUNNERS: Monday-Tuesday-Wednesday-Thursday at 6 to 7 A.M. take an easy 4-mile run at 7-minute to 8-minute pace.

STEEPLECHASE RUNNERS follow same pattern but do Monday's interval work over barriers at a pace two seconds slower on each lap.